Historical Problems:
Studies and Documents
Edited by
PROFESSOR G. R. ELTON
University of Cambridge

23

POLITICS AND THE PUBLIC CONSCIENCE

Slave Emancipation and the Abolitionist Movement in Britain

POLITICS AND THE PUBLIC CONSCIENCE

Slave Emancipation and the
Abolitionist Movement in Britain

Edith F. Hurwitz

Author of *Jamaica: A Historical Portrait*

LONDON: GEORGE ALLEN & UNWIN LTD
NEW YORK: BARNES & NOBLE BOOKS
(a division of Harper & Row Publishers, Inc.)

First Published in 1973

British ISBN 0 04 942116 6   HARDBACK
          0 04 942117 4   PAPERBACK

Published in the USA 1973 by
HARPER & ROW PUBLISHERS, INC.
BARNES & NOBLE IMPORT DIVISION

American ISBN 06-493076-9

Printed in Great Britain
in 10 on 11 pt Plantin type
by the Aldine Press, Letchworth

TO SAM
In Memoriam

PREFACE

The historian's quest carries with it an obligation to do more than merely reflect in the mirror of time the events of another age. In this study of a revolutionary event—slave emancipation in the British Empire—this historian has used her looking-glass not only to view the events connected with all aspects of the Anti-Slavery Movement, but to delve into their particular significance for British history and society.

In the process of sifting through the sources, order and coherence were created and a composite picture emerged of another time and place. This was the mental backdrop upon which this interpretative essay was drawn. Although not everything found was used in the final version, the information proved essential for developing an intuitive sense about the passions and concerns of another age. Thus rendered alert, I found myself able to probe more comprehensively the environment in which the event took place. Judgements concerning meaning and significance could be made. An evaluation of the past could be made for the present.

Thus the help of the very many libraries both in the United States and in Great Britain which provided resources for this project is gratefully acknowledged. In the United States, Cornell University's Slavery Collection was of singular importance. In 1871, Elizabeth Pease Nichol, Great Britain's leading feminine abolitionist, in an unusual gesture of transatlantic generosity gave her entire Anti-Slavery Library to that University. Thus in terms of printed literature, the Collection provided almost all the material needed for this study. I am grateful to the staff of the Rare Book Room and the Olin Library for providing helpful, friendly and efficient service.

Of the other American libraries the Friends' Historical Library of Swarthmore College, the Quaker Collection at Haverford College, the Perkins Library of Duke University, the Treavor Arnett Library of Atlanta University, the Boston Public Library (Boston, Massachusetts), the William L. Clements Library of the University of Michigan, the Brooklyn College Library, the University of Hawaii Library, the Columbia University Library and the New York Public Library must be thanked for providing either manuscript or printed source material.

In Great Britain, as with most historical projects, one must begin with the British Museum. Its Department of Manuscripts provided the Thomas Clarkson Papers, minute books of the Slave Trade Abolition Committee, and the Liverpool Papers Relating to the Slave Trade.

Of the University Libraries, St John's College, Cambridge, made available their collection of Thomas Clarkson correspondence. At

Oxford, there were the Anti-Slavery Papers at Rhodes House and the British Empire Manuscripts, Anti-Slavery Correspondence in the Department of Western Manuscripts, Bodleian Library. University College, London, provided correspondence by Thomas Clarkson, Thomas Fowell Buxton and Lord Brougham. Grateful thanks go to the librarians of those institutions for their informative service.

Of the other depositories in the British Isles, I give thanks to the John Rylands Library, Manchester, Dr Williams Library, London, the Ipswich Borough Libraries and the Wordsworth Library, Grasmere.

In 1966, a research fellowship from the Henry E. Huntington Library, San Marino, California, made it possible for me to examine their collection of Thomas Clarkson correspondence and the Family Papers of Zachary Macaulay. I owe special thanks to that important depository for its support.

To the National Endowment for the Humanities and the Committee on Afro-American Studies at Yale University, chaired during 1971–2 by John Blassingame, I owe a particular debt of gratitude. With the support of the committee I was awarded a research fellowship by the N.E.H. and became a Visiting Fellow at Yale. Thus I had the resources of Yale University at my disposal to do the final version of the manuscript. Additional thanks go to the helpful staff of the Afro-American Studies Department and the Sterling Memorial Library for their fine service.

Robin Winks, Cynthia Eagle Russett and David Brion Davis—members of the History Department, Yale University—helped by sharing common interests and by their stimulating reading of portions of the manuscript. Any errors of interpretation or fact which unintentionally remain are, of course, my own.

John Hope Franklin of the University of Chicago was generous in his support of all aspects of my work. Emily Hahn showed gratifying understanding for the effect that the pains of literary creation had on this author.

My children, Arthur Charles and Shelah Joyce, in their loving efforts to understand what their mother's book-writing was all about, provided that special help that only they know how to give. And last and most important, my husband, the late Samuel J. Hurwitz, is remembered always for the profound influence that he had on my life and work. Among the many things we shared with each other was the hope of re-creating the past on its own terms.

New Haven, Conn.   E.F.H.
January, 1973

CONTENTS

INTRODUCTION

Introduction

The success of the British Anti-Slavery Movement indicates that there have been moments in British history when values have taken precedence over economics, when the spiritual triumphed over the material. The vitality of British Protestantism and its relationship with the Protestant state account in large part for the success of the British Anti-Slavery Movement. Its denominations had been at various times in their history both radical and conservative, and in 1833 its radicalism assumed revolutionary proportions. This study attempts to explain the movement's ideological impact upon British society both in terms of the causes of its triumphs and the reasons for its popular success.

The rational yardstick which historians use to judge events can thus go so far and no further in explaining this phenomenon. The abolitionist movement coerced the political leaders, forcing men and parties to bow to their demands. A reform movement triumphed which based its appeal to the nation on the raw emotion of religious fervour.

The 'vitality' of the Anti-Slavery Movement and its ultimate successes can be viewed in the perspective of its evangelical dynamic. Its ideology called for action as well as pinning down an evil. If society was supporting an 'incalculable wrong' the movement's leaders were prepared to act against it.

For Christians who had lost faith in the revealed word of God, the slavery conflict was itself a revelation which reanimated religious symbols, providing a new sense of historical identity and purpose. Having its genesis in a Christian revival, the movement and its leaders continued to show the zeal of the convert for fundamental Christian truth. Because this regenerative truth, once grasped, seemed so self-evident, they shared an easy confidence in its ability to reform. Truth needs only to reach the heart for it quickly to dissolve all sin.

Hitherto historians who have dealt with the movement have collected its various threads into a single skein sometimes called humanitarianism and at other times called enlightened philanthropy. The eighteenth century's infatuation with the primitive, the noble savage, and its worship of benevolence have also been taken into account as factors essential for the birth of the Anti-Slavery crusade. Still another and more contemporary twist which attempts to refute these explanations was first expounded by Eric Williams in *Capitalism and Slavery* (1944). His thesis was that 'mature industrial capitalism' destroyed the slave system while the slave trade was abolished to protect the older British colonies in the Caribbean from the competition of newer colonies acquired by Britain as a result of the Napoleonic wars.

What all these views have failed to take into account is the character of the ideology which cast a critical eye on slavery. While it is true that the environment and the culture of the times had something to do with the acceptance of the values of the reformers, it was the more particular appeal of the Anti-Slavery Movement itself that determined the outcome of the cause. Thus arguments that the abolition of slavery came about as a result of the accommodation of class and economic interests, or because of certain cultural sensibilities and predispositions, fail to grasp the impact that ethical values, stemming from religious ideology, had on British society.

To go beyond and yet at the same time to take into account these more traditional factors of interpretation, David Brion Davis has developed the moral approach to the problem. Favoured in the past by W. E. H. Lecky, it has been subjected to the scrutiny of contemporary historical scholarship. Professor Davis believes that 'slavery has always been a source of social and psychological tension' in Western culture but that the 'underlying contradiction of slavery' really was made clear when 'the institution was closely linked with American colonization . . .'. Living with these conditions, Davis implies, motivated some men to seek reform. For Davis the 'Problem of Slavery in Western Culture' is a problem of the 'conflict of moral values' in history. It is also a problem of analysing the situational factors that determine the course of events that led individuals and groups to take up the cause of moral reform. Yet with it all there was also the question of individual commitment. As Davis notes: 'no matter how ripe the time, there would be no coalescing of anti-slavery opinion until specific decision and commitments were taken by individual men.'[1]

This study employs a conceptual framework similar to that of Professor Davis in that it assumes that slavery posed a moral conflict to the ideological traditions of Great Britain. It illustrates the interaction between ideology and individual commitment in its more specific British Protestant context. In terms of British society it places in a

[1] David Brion Davis, *The Problem of Slavery in Western Culture* (Ithaca, New York, 1966).

historical continuum the continuing clash between the value system of key constituents of the community and the activities of the Protestant state.

The approach has been to view the movement against slavery in the British Empire as an important example of the revitalization of moral values in a Christian culture. The ethical traditions of western civilization founded on the notion of an available and transcendental God who views all men as equal have throughout history been subverted by many forces. In the eighteenth and nineteenth centuries slavery both in its British and American contexts proved to be a most serious threat to these ethical values. It was the British nation through certain significant groups in its society that most effectively thwarted that challenge and arrested that threat. Thus this study will attempt to explain the conditions upon which a moral tradition, the underlying ethos of a Christian culture, can be shaped and moulded into a force for political achievement.

The eighteenth-century evangelical revival laid the foundation for a wide variety of Christian reform movements. William Wilberforce and his fellows at Clapham, and before them Wesley and Whitefield, initiated a new approach to spreading the gospels of Christianity by making them 'practically applicable to a wide variety of social problems and individual conflicts'. Dissenting religious denominations such as the Quakers, Baptists, Unitarians, Presbyterians and newly formed Methodists also sought to revitalize and rejuvenate their religious bodies by branching out into new areas of Christian expression for their members to participate in.

Reformers were on the verge of a brave new world; from the end of the eighteenth century and throughout the nineteenth century that world was formed slowly and surely with zeal and dedication. It was embraced by the British middle class as a result of lecturing, preaching, admonitions and the reading of the literature of reform. The call was out to accept God's boundless grace and for doing God's work on earth. Practical programmes of individual participation such as societies against gaming and for distributing the Bible were formed.

The evangelical voices behind these reforms whether they were Anglican or Dissenting assumed that similar reforms were possible in the slave colonies. For these were controlled by British subjects endowed with the qualities common to all other Englishmen in that they had the power as mortals to receive the grace of God. As the society that opposed vice advised Englishmen not to partake of it, so the abolitionists ultimately admonished British subjects to free themselves from supporting slavery.

The Anglican evangelicals under the leadership of Wilberforce with the backing of Nonconformist sects were impelled by the nature of the objectives of reform to bring their cause into the political arena. From 1787 on there was a new spirit of religion active in political protest, and its most enduring expression was found in the Anti-Slavery crusade. To the abolitionists and their followers slavery was a problem of morals; the slave was denied religion and prevented from worshipping God. Slavery kept Africans heathens when they could become Christians. Those who participated in slavery and the slave trade were therefore impeding God's work. 'You cannot exercise an improper dominion over a fellow creature', Thomas Clarkson declared, 'but by a wise ordering of providence you must necessarily injure yourself.' The goal of the abolitionists was to promote Christianity among those who had sinned by participating in slavery and the slave trade and among the Negro slaves who had been denied access to Christianity. All who joined the abolitionist fold became agents of God.

British abolitionists were sure that their reform proposals would win out only after they had converted the state and its citizens. Abolitionists did not wish to do away with the existing social order. They had a profound respect for the institutions of British society. As they saw it, the achievement of the goal of reform—abolition—was a fundamental method of conserving those institutions inasmuch as they were guardians of the moral order. As its aim was to reaffirm the values of society, the abolitionists' movement won the respect and loyalty of key constituents of the social order.

The political hierarchy of British society resisted many demands for reform in the nineteenth century. The values of classical liberalism, the image of a society of independent individuals free to pursue their callings uncoerced by the state, was the viewpoint that most often prevailed. Yet this value consensus was completely overthrown to accommodate the demands of Protestant communities for the abolition of slavery. This most daring use of state power was almost without precedent in all of British history. That the British state should deprive its most distinguished citizens of their property even if it was in human form was an unprecedented use of state power in any age and certainly in the age of liberalism. Though there were monetary compensations, the sacramental value that private property had in English common law was overturned.

This study will concentrate on the why and wherefore of slave emancipation. The political struggle over the slave trade has not been dealt with, because in terms of British history the Emancipation Act of 1833 was a far more radical piece of legislation than the abolition of the slave trade. After all, there had been, since at least the seventeenth century, a long tradition of the regulation of commerce by the British state. However, there was no precedent at all for an act of parliament that deprived important British citizens of their private property and then compensated them for it at great cost to the state. The Anti-Slavery Movement sought and secured the emancipation of 800,000 slaves in the British Empire.

At that moment in history, the Christian values of British tradition were given the sanctification not only of words but of deeds by the Protestant state. It was in Great Britain in 1833 that a political and ecclesiastical establishment, formed and operating through a consensus of well-established power relationships that had long supported not only the vested interests connected with slavery but also the values of property on which that institution was based, took the revolutionary step of doing away with them both.

Yet it is usually the 1832 Reform Bill which appears as the most discussed, analysed and dramatized event of the 1830s. In the perspective of time, however, the abolition of slavery by legislative statute reveals at least as much about the character of the British nation as does the Reform Bill. Was it perhaps the particular historic compromise between the established Anglican Church and Protestant Dissenters in 1688 which sowed the seeds for the abolition of the slavery in 1833; and which swung the state to an acceptance of moral equality?

The Emancipation Act might be considered as a forecasting of things to come. In an age of paternalism, in an age of empire, in an undemocratic age, it proclaimed a principle of equality. It is more than a century since that Emancipation Act, and in the passage of time many other movements of social reform have brought the British state to act on this principle. Yet it was in 1833 that it was first acknowledged because the enslaved African posed a challenge to the Christian conscience.

Like other milestones of history, the emancipation of the slaves came about as a result of a complex set of causes that created the historical moment at which this goal was achieved. There were long-range factors that had to do with the clash and conflict created in British society by the abolitionist movement. There were the political factors that had to do with the reform of parliament. And there were finally the many elements of chance, the many moments during the final stages of the struggle when the success of emancipation turned on the political tensions of the immediate conflict. There was also the role of individuals; the fate of slave emancipation might have been radically different had there not been Thomas Fowell Buxton and Edward

Stanley in key leadership positions. The study of this event does expose the limitations of historical inquiry. There can be little doubt, however, that the given nexus in time in which the campaign was waged set the stage for the revolutionary event. Whether history is made by individuals, social change created by chance events, long term considerations or a combination of all these, is cause for endless speculation about many crucial landmarks in history and surely is so in this case.

The purpose of my study, then, is to delineate the factors that made the Anti-Slavery Movement so successful. To dig into the roots of its passionate support. To attempt to ascertain the why and wherefore of the British government's adopting the goals of religious idealists. To set the crusade for the abolition of slavery against the larger perspective of British history and development. To determine whether the evaluation of W. E. H. Lecky, the nineteenth-century historian of moral development, holds for the historical perspective of today: 'The unweary, unostentatious, and inglorious crusade of England against slavery may probably be regarded as among the three or four perfectly virtuous pages comprised in the history of nations.'[2]

[2] *History of European Morals*, I, p. 153.

Ideological Trends in Anti-Slavery Thought

Great Britain, a Protestant nation, is host to and guardian of a Protestant culture. The Anti-Slavery ideology added another dimension to the definition of that culture. Its religious condemnation of slavery filtered into all institutions of British society. The specific ideological critique of the movement's leaders and propagandists was taken up by other concerned members of the Protestant community. To examine the ideology is to include not only the tracts and books of the leaders of the movement (and there was a considerable number of these) but those of theologians of many faiths and other concerned parties. However, it was the Anti-Slavery Movement which brought to the Protestant community the awareness of the realities of slavery, heightening its sense as to its wrongs. The Protestant imagination was stirred to intensive heights, to new expressions of symbolic Christian mythology, by the enormities of slavery.

To substantiate their critique they referred to the biblical tales of God's pronouncements concerning the behaviour of man. The attack on slavery was most often put in theological terms, both written and spoken. Oratorical phrases were couched in biblical cadence, giving them the weight and the authority, not only in meaning but in impact also, of hearing the word of a revealed God. Anti-Slavery audiences never tired of hearing the arguments repeated in exactly the same phrases. To them it was to experience again and again the impact of the holy spirit—to reaffirm with others the oneness of faith and to be strengthened against the ambiguities connected with the unknown dimension, the mystique of their God.

The traumatic effect that the ideology had on British Protestantism is a reflection of the particular stress that evangelicals put on the impact of revelation on the community. The ultimate in both individual and community expression was to acknowledge a revealed God, a God that was available to all men; a God that had boundless grace for all who would acknowledge his power. It was also a unique God, one who touched every individual in a particular manner. The collective conscience of a large number of British Protestants was polarized by the Anti-Slavery Movement because its ideology claimed to carry the revealed word of God.

The ideological development of the movement can be divided into two periods. During the period 1787–1807 its goal was not to emancipate the slaves but to abolish the slave trade. From 1823–33 the movement's objective was to abolish slavery. Common themes linked the ideology of both periods. Yet because of the differing objectives of the movement and the time span of more than a decade that elapsed between its major political campaigns, the literature emphasized and stressed different aspects of the polemic. Throughout, however, the underlying themes represented as a religious world view were continuous. The imperative need to bring God's spirit to all men was the most common theme.[1]

Service to God was a theme often emphasized by the earliest ideologues of the Anti-Slavery Movement. Granville Sharp, one of the first Anglicans publicly to attack slavery, developed an ethical rationale for this idea based on natural law. For Sharp the first law of nature was that man lives by the commands of God. In a tract *On The Law of Nature and Principal Action in Man* Sharp views man as motivated by the commands of God. His actions are based on them. If man wishes to claim the glorious privileges that God provides in this world and the life to come he lives by the 'Royal Law' which Sharp here calls the 'Rule of Obedience'. Man is forever checking his own self-interest, curbing it and putting it down. To those who believe that we are motivated by self-love Sharp answers that though 'self-love is the main branch of the law of nature' (that is a part of all of us), yet through our conscience we subordinate this feeling to the 'rule of obedience'. God's rule is to subordinate our self-interest to the needs of the community. Believing that this rule is embedded in the conscience, Sharp was certain that every man had the ability to determine what was proper behaviour.

Sharp's argument introduces a second theme common in Anti-Slavery ideology—retribution. Sharp points to the West Indian planter who justifies slavery in terms of self-interest. He feels as one who fails to obey the 'rule of obedience' that no wrong is done by depriving the

---

[1] For a brilliant and path-breaking discussion of Anti-Slavery thought see David Brion Davis, *The Problem of Slavery in Western Culture* (London, 1971; New York, 1966).

Negro. He cannot subordinate his self-interest. A nature that cannot subordinate self-interest becomes overrun with pride. Proud behaviour will bring severe sanctions from God. In the past it 'brought the fall of Satan himself'. Many in England risk this downfall because there is great support for 'the most abominable oppression that ever disgraced man-kind: the African slave trade and tolerance of slavery in the British Colonies'.[2] Through his 'rule of obedience' which was the 'golden rule' Sharp asked man to do what all evangelicals believed man should do, i.e. transcend the basic self-love that all have for a higher love, so that man will be able to live by the 'rule of obedience'— God's command. No man can make another his property because we owe our creation to God, the ruler of the universe. It is the Christian master who is 'guilty of sacrilege' by appropriating to himself a life which 'peculiarly belongs to God by an inestimable purchase'. It is contrary to the natural order of the universe to demand the ownership of another man. The slaveholder and African trader displayed 'unnatural pretensions' as they persisted in holding in 'absolute property their poor bretheren . . .'.[3] Sharp's ideas on the motivation of man's actions were very much in the Protestant evangelical tradition which identified the very nature of sin in terms of self-interest and self-centeredness.

An identical theme pervaded the work of John Wesley, founder of Methodism. His 1774 pamphlet, *Thoughts On Slavery*, was a critique of the failure of those involved in slavery to seek out and discover the nature of God's demand. Those who were enslaved and those who did the enslaving rejected a relationship between themselves and God. They had not received his grace through conversion. The possibility was ever present, however, to reform the situation. Man must resolve to love instead of hate and once that resolution is taken there will be peace with God and love in the heart of man. An awareness of the natural capacity to love is given to all men through God. It can flower forth and be cultivated.

The just God will reward every man according to his works. Like Sharp, Wesley believed that God's wrath would afflict those who cannot love and who show no compassion for their fellow men. 'He shall have judgment without mercy, that showed no mercy.' Yet there was always the ability within man to change and become one with God, to find grace. The transformation of God's anger into love was ever a possibility.

[2] *On the Law of Nature and Principal Action in Man* (London, 1776), pp. 204–5.
[3] Granville Sharp, *The Law of Liberty or Royal Law by Which All Mankind Will Certainly Be Judged* (London, 1776), pp. 18–36.

When the hearts of those involved in slavery relented Wesley believed that it was because of the 'call from God for love'.[4]

The Quaker Anthony Benezet, whose 1782 tract, *An Historical Account of Guinea*, had considerably influenced Wesley's outlook on slavery, led a transatlantic crusade against the oppression. In his 1754 Philadelphia Meeting his personal crusade to divest Quakers of slavery began. In 1766 he issued *A Caution and Warning to Great Britain and Her Colonies* in America and forwarded two thousand copies of this book to Friends in London, requesting that it be placed in the hands of British officials. Benezet also corresponded with Granville Sharp and introduced him to still another American Quaker abolitionist, Dr Benjamin Rush. As a subject of the British Empire, Benezet carried his crusade to the centre of its power by enlisting the support of English friends. He also helped to build the alliance between like-minded Anglicans and Friends that would be at the core of the Anti-Slavery crusade.

Quaker theology had long expressed the belief in God's spirit in every man; that in all men's souls there shone a light from God. Inherent in the spirit of man was the seed of God ready to work on the soul. Benezet's *Caution* of 1766 denounced slavery for destroying the bonds 'of natural affection and interest, whereby mankind in general are united' by God. Speaking of the Quaker theology in general Benezet in 1780 declared that the 'gift of saving light and grace hath appeared to all men'.[5]

God's precepts are in every man and they must be discovered by every individual so that he may live by them. Moral behaviour springs from this, and one need not be hampered by dogmatic theology in finding God. The evangelicalism of Wesley and the theology of Quakers such as Benezet were one in their belief in the immediate and emotional way in which God reveals himself to all men.[6]

Baptists shared this ideological view of slavery and the slave trade. They were still another group of Dissenters that supported the Anti-Slavery crusade. Abraham Booth, their leading theologican, denounced slavery in a tract published in 1788. As was true of the others he believed in the universal nature of grace. It was a spiritual feeling 'suited for the

[4] John Wesley, *Thoughts On Slavery* (London, 1774), pp. 46–7. For a discussion of Sharp and Wesley in terms of Protestant thought see Davis, *Problem*, pp. 385–6.

[5] Anthony Benezet, *A Caution and Warning To Great Britain And Her Colonies*. Edward Grubb, *Quaker Thought and History* (New York, 1925), p. 36. George S. Brooks, *Friend Anthony Benezet* (Philadelphia, 1937), p. 82.

[6] Davis, *Problem*, p. 306. Frederick Tolles, *Quakers and the Atlantic Culture* (New York, 1960), pp. 104–13.

state of enlightened mind, to the feelings of awakened conscience and to the desires of renewed heart'. God was all forgiving of past transgressions. Booth pointed to the universals in the relationships of all men. There could be no doubt that 'sable bondmen and their brother Africans' were comprehended in the 'one blood' of which 'God hath made all nations'. Being of that blood they were subjected to 'the same divine principles, and holy affections, and spiritual joys, and heavenly hopes, with themselves'. Booth was distressed at the idea that British Christians thought the African to be a world apart.[7]

Anti-Slavery ideologues of all denominations shared the view of society that saw man as governed by natural laws which guided his behaviour. This gave men a vital core of autonomy and self-direction. Moral freedom was defined in terms of the 'lack of dependence upon the will of others, in the natural exercise of the human faculties, and in the unfettered pursuit of enlightened self-interest'. Locke's view that society is composed of discrete, self-governing individuals, whose true humanity lay in the proprietorship of their persons, permeated Anti-Slavery thought.

One of the eighteenth century's most popular explanations of natural laws was contained in the moral philosophy of William Paley. First published in 1785 the book had ten editions and was the official text on ethics at Cambridge. Paley's definitions of the governing laws of mankind were widely in use as guides to the individual's behaviour in the social order. Man's natural rights according to his text were the right to 'life, limbs and liberty: his rights to the produce of his personal labour; to the use of in common with others, of air, light, water'. Persons drawn from all over who found themselves on a desert island would be entitled to these rights. Discussing benevolence Paley believed that 'God wills and wishes the happiness of his creatures'. Human conduct therefore must be judged in terms of whether it fulfils his expectations.

Slavery and the slave trade violated these rights. Paley proposed in a rare public statement on a topical issue that the trade be abolished and the slaves gradually emancipated. Through the mild diffusion of Christianity men will perceive the wickedness of slavery. The rights of mankind were reciprocal, as there were mutual obligations of a moral nature between men. Paley's view of the trade and slavery was an important support for abolitionists. He corresponded with Clarkson

---

[7] Abraham Booth, *Commerce of Human Species and The Enslaving of Innocent Persons Inimical to the Laws of Moses and The Gospel of Christ*, 3rd edn (London, 1792), pp. 33, 98–9. Joseph Priestly, the prominent Unitarian theologian, expressed the same ideas in *A Sermon On The Subject Of The Slave Trade Delivered To A Society of Protestant Dissenters* (Birmingham, 1788).

who considered him to be a 'coadjutor in interesting the mind of the public in favour of the oppressed Africans'.[8]

The arguments of the first generations of Anti-Slavery ideologues would be summoned once again by a new generation of Anti-Slavery propagandists when the political goals of the movement became focused on the radical goal of emancipation. The continuities in thought between the generations in the movement are striking. They repeatedly returned to the evangelical credo as their basic reason for justifying the goal of the movement—complete emancipation.

A synthesis of the traditional Anti-Slavery ideology recast in terms of the contemporary problems was the Baptist theologian Benjamin Godwin's *Lectures On Slavery* (1830). Godwin discussed the laws of God and man. The Negro was treated like a brute, yet no man could be a brute because he has a mind, an immaterial spirit, an immortal soul. These faculties of man enable him to acquire knowledge, judge right and wrong, govern the appetite of his body, and search for the wonders of nature. It is also within every man to perceive the glories of the creator, the wonders of redeeming mercy and to have communication with God so as to be prepared through instruction and moral discipline for the 'sublime enjoyments of the heavenly state'. The laws of God and all human laws are founded in justice.

Thus slavery was against the British constitution as well, because it too was founded on the laws of nature and justice to fellow creatures. Referring to Blackstone, Godwin declares that the laws of the constitution are the same 'eternal, immutable laws of good and evil which the creator in all his dispensations conforms'.[9]

Still another theme of major importance in Anti-Slavery ideology was centred around the attributes of the Negro character. If God's grace was boundless and available to all, Anti-Slavery writesr had to emphasize the qualities in the Negro character that would make him particularly receptive to accept love and forgiveness from God. If he were aggressive and combative as his oppressors claimed he was then the Negro might be thought of as beyond redemption. Anti-Slavery writers described African personality in positive terms. Their image of the Negro was supported by contemporary writers. If the

[8] Davis, *Problem*, p. 412. Thomas Clarkson, *The History of The Rise, Progress and Accomplishment of the Abolition of The African Slave Trade By The British Parliament*, 2 vols (London, 1808), vol. I, p. 194. *The Works of William Paley*, 5 vols (Cambridge, 1830), vol. III, pp. 35, 43. In vol. V, Paley's attack on slavery is in a 'Speech On The Abolition of The Slave Trade Delivered at a Meeting of the Inhabitants of Carlisle', 9 February 1792.

[9] Benjamin Godwin, *Lectures On Slavery* (Boston, 1836), pp. 54, 104.

African was truly like every other man then the oppressive environment
that he came from could not change his innate nature. In the course of
the eighteenth century the 'great question then was whether the literary
imagination could build a bridge of sympathy and understanding
across the enormous gulf that divided primitive and civilized cultures'.[10]

Anthony Benezet was the first ideologue of the Anti-Slavery movement to strike an effective synthesis between a purely rational argument
based on what was thought to be objective environmental evidence and
a subjective appeal in terms of moral and religious progress. Writing
in 1807 after the slave trade had been abolished, Thomas Clarkson
named Benezet as the important intellectual of the movement. A
synthesis of rational argument with evangelical fervour, *An Historical
Account of Guinea*, had an important popular appeal. 'It became instrumental, beyond any other book ever before published, in disseminating
a proper knowledge and detestation of this trade.'

Benezet wrote the model tract. Arguments against colonial slavery
would always be based on a careful examination of the evidence at hand
that proved it evil. At the same time, the ultimate religious meaning of
these events would never be overlooked and would always be evaluated
with equal emphasis and importance. It was the intrusion of European
society into Africa that spoiled its civilization.

Benezet's argument was an environmental one. God has given men
different areas on the face of the earth to inhabit according to their
different personalities. Though Guinea is not a conducive environment
for Europeans who do not remain healthy there, for the Negroes it is
ideal. They enjoy a good state of health. Throughout the tract, Benezet
cited books, articles and travel accounts as evidence to support his
assertions concerning the African character. It was in part an anthology
of readings about Africa and in part a polemic against slavery.[11] Benezet
and the literary cult of the primitive in the eighteenth century had
defined African character in a positive light.

To rally popular support behind the final measures instituted in
parliament to abolish the slave trade, William Wilberforce in 1807
addressed himself to the question of the Negro character, using similar
arguments as those put forth by earlier publicists. For him it was a
fundamental question. He acknowledged that the arguments used by the
'advocates of the slave trade originally took very high ground'. To their
contention that the Negro was of an inferior race of brutes, the abolitionists had shown that this was a 'shameless position'. African civilization

[10] Davis, *Problem*, pp. 473–4.
[11] Clarkson, *History*, vol. I, p. 169. John Wesley used Benezet's approach in
his *On Slavery* and depicted African personality as being unspoilt and uncorrupt.

was not distinctly inferior and its people did have the intellectual powers of European man.

Authoritative sources were used by Wilberforce to sustain his position. As Benezet had done almost thirty-five years before, Wilberforce cited travel accounts of visitors to Africa who had observed the race in its native environment. Two of the accounts he used were written by those who supported the institution of slavery, so that they could not be branded as abolitionist propaganda. The view presented was that of a superior civilization:

> of their almost universal benevolence, gentleness, and hospitality; of their courage and, when they have an adequate motive to prompt them to work, of their industry and perseverance; of their parental and filial tenderness, of their social and domestic affection, of the conjugal fidelity of the women, combined with great cheerfulness and frankness ... scarcely inferior to any thing which is recorded in Greek or Roman story.

Having marshalled fresh and revealing evidence that the African character was equal if not superior to the European, Wilberforce next addressed himself to the question of African society. Drawing parallels between British and African development he noted that Great Britain was isolated and just as much in an inferior state of development when Rome first reached her. Africa had been isolated from similar contacts with more advanced civilization: hence the differences in her development. And such contact as there has been so far 'instead of polishing and improving, has tended not merely to retard her natural progress' but to 'barbarize her wretched inhabitants'. In Africa the countries on the coast that have had most contact with Europeans are in the greatest state of barbarism, while the ones isolated and situated in the interior 'are far more advanced in the comforts and improvements of social life.'[12]

Thus the Anti-Slavery forces countered the pro-slavery image of Africa with a very positive picture of their own. Their concern for the African was centred not only in America but on his native continent as well. Wilberforce and others blamed the slave trade for destroying the fabric of African society. They believed that once the slave trade was abolished, the states there could proceed to develop economically, socially, morally and politically. Great Britain should develop a legitimate trade that would foster economic relations alternative to those based on the buying and selling of people. England could play an important

---

[12] William Wilberforce, *A Letter On The Abolition of the Slave Trade* (London, 1807), pp. 63–4, 66–7, 71–2, 86–7.

role in bringing African civilization into the orbit of the West. To put these plans into practice the leaders of the Anti-Slavery Movement organized in 1807 a society that would oversee the development of Africa. On 14 April 1807 the African Institution was formed.[13]

Between 1788 and 1807 abolitionists had drawn together an all-encompassing plan for the development of the African race that took into account both their native land and their foreign territories of captivity. Confident that the abolition of the slave trade had removed a great obstacle to African continental improvement, they hoped to guide things along with the African Institution and through the direct contact of the missionary societies.

Abolitionist spokesmen during the following decades would make every effort to impart information to the public concerning the problems of the Negro race both in Africa and in the New World. As they would promote African development, they would with equal care and considerably more attention look to the slave societies of the British Empire with the hope of reforming them.

In ideological terms, Benezet, Sharp and many others who denounced slavery in the eighteenth century were committed to doing away with it completely. Sharp worked with the committee organized in 1787 to abolish the slave trade. When it came to creating a political issue, he like the others was ready to settle for more limited objectives.

Fearful of disturbing the social order, they did not seek radical alternatives in 1807. Rather they hoped to reform the slave society instead. Their programme had the approval of those who had lived in the slave society. William Dickson, a former colonial official in Barbados, wrote a book called *Mitigation of Slavery* which was published with the support of the Slave Trade Abolition Committee in 1814. Dickson discussed the successful efforts of Joshua Steele, a prominent planter in Barbados, to improve the lot of his slaves. Though Steele's reforms and Dickson's suggestions were highly impracticable in 1814, the book did bring the problem of slavery and the slave society to the attention of the public at large at a time when the abolitionists were devoting much of their energy to international efforts to abolish the slave trade.[14]

Related to that problem was the slave registration system proposed

[13] Clarkson, *History*, vol. I, p. 12. Ralph Austen and Woodruff Smith, 'Images of Africa and British Slave Trade Abolition: the Transition to Imperialist Ideology,' *African Historical Studies*, vol. II (1969), pp. 69–83.

[14] Wilberforce, *A Letter*, pp. 176–7. Thomas Birtwhistle, 'The Development of Abolitionism, 1807–23' (unpublished M.A. thesis, London University, 1948), p. 58, Bibliography.

by James Stephen in 1812 to effectively control the illicit imports of slaves into the West Indian islands. It was used in Trinidad from 1812: soon after Wilberforce proposed in parliament that a registration system be established for all British colonies. If the system was put into practice, abolitionists hoped that the planters would feel obligated to reform conditions. If the government kept an account of the number of slaves in their plantations, harsh treatment could be checked. The registry as an instrument of supervision would further aid the reformation of the slave society. As George Stephen pointed out, it was a means by which the 'true condition of the colonial negroes' could be made a 'matter of public, notorious, and conclusive evidence'. Slave registration was adopted in all the colonies.[15]

By 1820 abolitionists had become disillusioned with their reform programme. They were less hopeful about the probability of reforming the slave society from within. Neither the abolition of the slave trade nor the slave registration scheme had been effective tools for changing the attitudes of the local elites. Registry returns were incomplete and the laws of the colonies reflected a decided hostility towards the amelioration of the conditions of slave life. Missionaries that had been sent out by non-conformist sects in increasing numbers since the first decades of the nineteenth century were receiving a hostile welcome in the colonies. The abolitionists were further dismayed by the failure of Great Britain to secure the international abolition of the slave trade.

A new approach was devised. The root of all evil—the institution of slavery itself—would be abolished. Immediate emancipation was not their goal. Their aim, as described by Sir Thomas Fowell Buxton, was 'not the sudden emancipation of the Negro; but such preparatory steps, such measures of precaution, as by slow degrees, and in a course of years, first fitting and qualifying the slaves for freedom, shall gently conduct us to the annihilation of slavery'. Without immediately infringing on the institution of slavery they hoped to reform it—to somehow change the attitude of the planter towards the slave without changing their basic relationship.[16]

Abolitionists came to accept the notion of emancipation as an ultimate good but in 1823 they were far from ready to have the slaves freed. Their commitment to emancipation was in the abstract rather than the concrete. With this long range goal in mind, they could overcome their

[15] James Stephen, *Reasons For Establishing A Registry of Slaves In The British Colonies* (London, 1815). George Stephen, *Anti-Slavery Recollections* (London, 1859), pp. 18–19.
[16] Charles Buxton (ed.), *Memoirs of Sir Thomas Fowell Buxton*, 3rd edn (London, 1849), p. 113.

general feelings of disillusionment about the failure of reform in the colonies.

Both the British nation and the slave society must be prepared for this most radical of alternatives. A programme was devised to secure the commitment of the Tory government to a goal of emancipation. It was to be brought about gradually through varying stages of reform. The new programme was introduced by Buxton on 15 May 1823 when he put a motion before parliament that 'the state of slavery is repugnant to the principles of the British constitution and of the Christian religion, and that it ought to be gradually abolished throughout the British colonies'.[17]

The British government under Canning, pressed by the abolitionists who demanded reforms and by the colonists who insisted that private property and the principle of local self-government could not be interfered with, sought to meet the demands of both sides by attempting to persuade the West Indian colonies to institute 'voluntary' reforms on a local level and thus avoid intervention by the imperial government. The West India Interest in parliament, recognizing that the attacks on slavery could best be resisted by ameliorating the conditions of the slaves, endorsed Canning's proposals. The survival of the institution of slavery could best be insured by a recognition—and reform—of its worst features and an imaginative defence which would call upon both emotion and reason.

With the support of the West Indian interests in parliament, the Tory government was quite justified in believing that the colonial legislatures could carry forward the programme of amelioration. A dispatch was sent to the colonial governors on 28 May 1823, instructing them to advise the colonial legislatures to enact measures to improve conditions for the slaves. Their reaction to this plan—decidedly reactionary and hostile—explains much about the future course of events.[18]

Zachary Macaulay, while alarmed at the colonial reaction to the amelioration proposals, knew that this was typically their pattern as they had behaved in a similar manner in 1807. 'No evil appears to them so great and hence their clamour on the present and former occasions.'[19] The government's proposals which were unanimously endorsed by parliament in May 1823 held no promise of emancipation nor did they

---

[17] Hansard, *Parliamentary Debates* n.s. IX, p. 257.

[18] For a discussion of the impact of these events on Jamaica see Samuel J. and Edith F. Hurwitz, *Jamaica: A Historical Portrait* (London, 1972; New York, 1971), ch. 5.

[19] Zachary Macaulay to William Cunningham, 10 February 1824, Macaulay Family Papers, Huntington Library, San Marino, California.

go as far in their reform programme as the abolitionists would have wished. Yet, by committing the British state to a programme of intervention in the affairs of the colonies, an important precedent had been established.

The recommendations of the imperial government could only be thought of as revolutionary by those who were responsible for, and lived in the midst of, the slave labour system. The suggestion that a slave's evidence be admitted in the courts of the island was considered particularly dangerous. As one member of the Jamaica Legislature put it in 1825:

> Can any measure be adopted which would have the effect of depressing the character of the higher classes and elevating the lower it would be admitting slave evidence. What could our enemies devise which would more effectually destroy the high feeling of superiority with which the white population are regarded than to place their lives and liberties at the mercy of slave evidence.

Jamaica's example was not lost on the other West Indian islands. An exasperated Colonial Secretary, the Earl of Bathurst, complained that they made the example of Jamaica 'their apology for doing so little'. Yet the British government was not eager to take up the challenge and could only counsel patience to those who demanded that stronger steps be taken against the recalcitrant wayward colonies.[20]

Once again events occurred that confirmed beyond doubt the abolitionists fears that the slave society could not reform itself. Moral sensibilities had been inflamed by the flagrant disregard for justice that the colonial governments had already shown not only towards the slaves but towards the missionaries. Some men within the ranks of the movement and even some of its leaders began to abandon their gradualist approach. In March 1825, Zachary Macaulay, secretary to the London Committee of the Anti-Slavery Society, reported that 'there has been much discussion and much correspondence among Anti-Slavery folks in London and in various parts of the country' about a new course of action.[21]

Thus the shift to immediatism—that is the demand for the immediate abolition of slavery—was being taken with ever greater determination by abolitionist followers in the countryside in 1825-6. Leaders, forced to respond to the demands of their followers, became aware that they

[20] Samuel J. and Edith F. Hurwitz, *Jamaica*, pp. 106–7.
[21] Zachary Macaulay to Henry Brougham, 25th March 1825, Macaulay Family Papers, Huntington Library. David Brion Davis, 'The Emergence of Immediatism in British and American Anti-Slavery Thought,' *Journal of American History*, vol. XLIX, no. 2, p. 220.

would have to push for more radical alternatives. Yet they moved cautiously, fearful as they were of sudden change. The 'gradualist mentality' dominated their outlook. Political events both at home and in the colonies would have a decisive influence on wiping away their gradualist approach.[22]

Convinced by every turn of events that the amelioration programme was doomed in the colonies, abolitionists continued to make this known to the public at large, not only in Parliament but through a new magazine, the *Anti-Slavery Reporter*, edited by Zachary Macaulay, which commenced publication in 1826. 'Alive to everything' he 'maintained a continual fire on the enemy'. In an article published in the 31 July 1826 issue of the *Reporter* the amelioration programme was scrutinized, criticized and torn apart.

Anxious as the abolitionist forces were for change, they still tied emancipation to gradual reform. The British government had supported that idea, and its authority could not easily be overcome. 'Colonial abuses, colonial obduracy, colonial hypocrisy were the only topics for agitation, but colonial castigation and colonial emancipation were tabooed.' Amelioration of conditions of slavery continued to be the government's policy.[23]

Meanwhile Anti-Slavery ideologues lashed out against the colour prejudice of the slave society. They had nothing but harsh criticism for the discriminatory practices that existed against the free Negroes in the colonies. To them it was a grave contradiction to be deprived of the rights of freemen because your skin colour linked you with a slave ancestry. Colour was a mark of oppression even for those who by legal definition were no longer oppressed. James Stephen believed they were victims of 'absurd political jealousies' and 'practical degradation' because they were held in complete contempt because of the colour of their skin. Stephen further explained that they were relegated to an inferior order in society which made the gap between the poorest peasant and the nobility seem minor by comparison. The distance would remain great, he argued, as 'the whites desired to maintain their profitable privileges and pre-eminence' by keeping the oppressive distinctions that separated the two groups.[24]

Abolitionists thought of the free Negro question as a major concern

[22] Davis, ibid., p. 216.
[23] George Stephen, *Anti-Slavery Recollections*, pp. 98–9.
[24] *The Slavery In The British West Indies Delineated* (London, 1824–30), vol. I, pp. 184, 429. Godwin, *Lectures*, pp. 106–7. Andrew Thomson, *Immediate Emancipation: Substance of a Speech Delivered at Edinburgh On October 19, 1830* (Edinburgh, 1830), pp. 37–8.

throughout the 1820s. One of the reforms of the slave society that they most ardently fought for during that period was to end the discriminatory practices against them. Thomas F. Buxton pointed to the great efforts of Henry Brougham and Stephen Lushington to rescue the free Negroes from their painful position. On 12 June 1827 Lushington was the spokesman in a debate on their condition in the House of Commons. He concentrated his attack on conditions in Jamaica, as this island had the largest free Negro population in the British Colonies and members of that community had petitioned parliament directly for the end of their second class status. Henry Brougham remarked upon the divisive nature of colour prejudice. 'These regulations had raised a barrier between two divisions of the human race; a partition wall had been erected.'[25]

Throughout the crusade and up until 1830 abolitionists in parliament had done what was expedient. They had continued to support a government policy of amelioration which was not calculated to disturb the status quo in any fundamental way in the colonies. They had been well aware that as long as the political power of the slave society remained in the hands of those who controlled the Negroes there could be little hope of meaningful change. Exhortation had moved the government but little. Canning's sudden death in 1827 brought things to a standstill. The new prime minister, the Duke of Wellington, was an arch conservative. The demands of the Anti-Slavery forces were met with rebuke. Wellington advised his colonial secretary Sir George Murray to send new instructions to the colonial governors to implement the amelioration principles first used in the Trinidad Order of Council of 1812. He was determined to keep the status quo on the slavery issue, and Anti-Slavery forces were aware that there was little they could do to change the situation.[26]

Abolitionists were frustrated in their attempts to assimilate what could be described as two dialectically opposite concepts. They had always pointed to the sinful nature of slavery; they tolerated that sin in the hope that slavery would do away with itself, under proper guidance. In 1823 Wilberforce recalled that he was often asked in the years 1789–1807 why the abolitionists did not press for the immediate extinction of

[25] Hansard, *Parliamentary Debates* n.s. XVII, pp. 1242–56. Edith F. Hurwitz 'The Struggle of the Free Negroes of Jamaica to Attain Political Rights 1711–1830' (unpublished M.A. Thesis, Brooklyn College, City University of New York, 1965), discusses the debate and its impact on the British government.

[26] Chester W. New, *Life of Henry Brougham to 1830* (London, 1961), ch. XV. William L. Mathieson, *British Slavery and its Abolition 1823–1838* (London, 1926), p. 193. David Brion Davis, 'James Cropper and the British Anti-slavery Movement 1823–1833', *Journal of Negro History*, vol. 46, pp. 163–4.

slavery instead of the abolition of the slave trade. It was the reasoning he remarked 'of many of our greatest and ablest opponents, as well as some of our warmest friends'. He questioned the past approach in a tract which was an appeal for emancipation. In retrospect he failed to understand the reasons for their cautious policy (Doc. 1).

There exists within Puritanism (as R. H. Tawney has noted) 'an element which was conservative and traditionalist, and an element which was revolutionary . . . a sober prudence which would garner the fruits of this world, and a divine recklessness which would make all things new.' It was these tendencies which found expression in Wilberforce's thoughts and in the ideas of other Anti-Slavery leaders. For twenty-five years they coped with their moral concern over the abuses of slavery. However after 1823 the reckless and revolutionary came to the fore and began to erode that caution. These 'rival tendencies in the soul of Puritanism itself' must be grasped, Tawney believes, if we are to understand why its ideology can go from one extreme to another.[27]

In the second period of intense abolitionist activity, 1830 to 1833, when the most radical solution of all—emancipation—became the cry of the crusaders, once again the principles of faith, the view of the relationship between God and man and the violation of it through slavery became the cry of those who denounced it. The movement's faith in the natural benevolence of men was severely shaken by the failure of those involved in slavery to reform. Earlier they had called upon them to repent, believing that they need only point out the evil and all would see the light. As their own conversions had given them absolute assurance of God's love, they confidently assumed that all men wished to be enlightened through knowledge and understanding. Yet the slave owner had failed to find within himself the spirit of God which translated into benevolent acts would have caused a change in his treatment of the slave. Therefore the relationship between master and slave had to be done away with. The property relationship which was contrary to the notion of universal equality of all men had to be abolished. Christians who in an earlier era had thought the amelioration of the slave system the road to meaningful reform were radicalized and advocated revolutionary solutions. Those who held the power in the system remained unregenerate. Therefore the basis of their power, the property relationship, had to be done away with. Exhortation had failed, revolutionary change was required.

[27] R. H. Tawney, *Religion and the Rise of Capitalism* (London, 1926, reprint 1962), p. 212. William Wilberforce, *An Appeal to the Religion, Justice, and Humanity of the Inhabitants of the British Empire on Behalf of the Negro Slaves* (London, 1823), pp. 5–6.

James Stephen was the first from among the original leaders to break completely with gradualism. Since this was radical departure from his other view, he had to justify his decision at length. He felt compelled to prove beyond doubt that the conditions in the slave society were so repressive that they stifled for ever the moral feeling of all men. In taking a position for immediate emancipation he felt like any immediatist that 'unless stifling and coercive influences were swept away, there could be no development of the inner controls of conscience, emulation, and self-respect, on which a free and christian society depended'.[28]

His *The Slavery In The British West Indies Delineated,* two massive volumes, the first of which appeared in 1824 and the second in 1830, represented a detailed and exhaustive analysis of the legal structure of the slave society and its labour practices. The first volume with appendices had nearly five hundred pages and discussed the legal sanctions that defined the relationship between master, slave and the political order of the slave society. While Stephen carefully pointed to the social controls of the slave society as being a bar to effective reform, he made no plea in the first volume for emancipation. His only conclusion was that 'I invoke on their behalf the wisdom, and justice of parliament, and the voice of a generous people.' When the second volume appeared in 1830 he had become committed to emancipation. In the book he showed the ways in which the oppression of the system affected the working life of the slave. In the concluding chapter he summarized the efforts of the abolitionist movement since 1807. 'We have progressively receded from those sacred principles of penitence and reformation, on which the abolitionist act was founded.' Justifying his plea for immediate emancipation on rational grounds he concluded impatiently that 'enough was known before; more than enough was incontrovertibly proved; nay, nay, enough was always admitted or undenied; to make the legislatures' tolerance of slavery a disgrace to the British and Christian name'.

For Stephen the justification for emancipation and the change in the social order that it would bring about was based on 'the best human safeguard of social order, the moral and religious belief of the people'! By 1830 the commitment of the rank and file of the Anti-Slavery Movement to immediate emancipation was justification enough for radical change.[29]

Stephen evinced much less determination when discussing the details of carrying out the emancipation of the slaves. Of all the Anti-Slavery leaders, he had been most inventive in offering amelioration schemes.

---

[28] Davis, *J.A.H.,* vol. XLIX, p. 229.
[29] James Stephen, *Slavery,* vol. II, pp. 387, 397, 413, 438.

Yet when it came to dealing with the greatest problem of all, he was stymied. The rational approach to the evils of slavery melted away before the grand ideal of freedom itself. The act of freeing the slaves was all that Stephen felt able to propose.

Like Stephen, Benjamin Godwin was against making specific proposals for emancipation. He looked at the question of immediate emancipation in his *Lectures On Slavery*. There was general agreement that the Negro's freedom should be granted 'not at some distant time, but now'. Many who advocate this 'prefer some plan of gradual abolition more or less speedy'. To those who feared violence should emancipation be immediately achieved, Godwin answered that there was no justification for these fears. Was there not 'something unnatural in the supposition, that by bestowing on a body of men a most important blessing, we should fire them with rage and indignation'. Amelioration and reform of the slave society had already been proven to be impossible. To free children, infants and women would be fraught with all types of difficulties. It had been proven beyond doubt that this evil needed to be removed. There had already been too many compromises; the principle of freedom versus bondage was now to be decided, oppression versus liberty. Like Stephen, Godwin felt that it was up to the government to create the emancipation plan so that the nation as a whole could be united behind it. All efforts must be directed to the extinction of slavery 'as early as the adoption of the necessary measures, and the carrying into effect will allow'.[30]

Godwin's and Stephen's predicament was characteristic of the Anti-Slavery leaders in 1830. They had reached an impasse and were forced to revise their views on the time-table for emancipation. Throughout the 1820s provincial Anti-Slavery societies had committed themselves to immediate emancipation, and in 1830 the annual London meeting had done the same. The fusion of theory, of ideology with a practical plan for action had given the Anti-Slavery Movement its dynamic thrust. By 1830 the plan first devised in 1788 and subsequently revised in 1811 and 1823 to reform the slave society was no longer practical. The list of priorities had to be revised and immediate emancipation headed the list. Yet Anti-Slavery leaders had been so fearful of taking this final step that they had not devised any concrete plan for emancipation. Agitators instead continued to concentrate their attack on the defects of the slave society.

To answer and refute the charges of the agitators employed by the Agency Committee, the pro-slavery forces sent out speakers to debate

[30] Godwin, *Lectures*, pp. 228, 242.

with the Anti-Slavery speakers. In 1832–3 the pro-slavery forces argued at public meetings that ancient Israelite slavery was in fact not a crime nor was it sinful because it had been permitted to exist under the sanction of God: God cannot sanction sin, therefore slavery is not sinful.

Abolitionist speakers answered this challenge by highlighting with dramatic oratorical strokes the radical differences between ancient Hebraic slavery and modern British slavery. Returning to their evangelical-fundamentalist adherence to the supreme authority of the Bible, they analysed ancient Hebrew slavery. In their speeches they demonstrated that modern slavery as practised in the colonies was far more oppressive and sinful than the forms practised by the Hebrews. These arguments appeared most often at a crucial juncture in the movement's history: 1830–2.

Addressing the ladies of Glasgow in 1833 George Thompson showed that the slavery of the Jews was not the same as that of British colonial slavery. God sanctioned it because the nations that were enslaved had been heathen: 'filled up by the measures of their sins, and against whom the wrath of God was revealed even unto death.' Jews lived by the laws of God and by knowledge of his moral and providential government. Hence the slaves they held were not degraded as were those in the West Indies. They merely had to pay tribute to the Jews and were free to pursue their individual lives. They were treated with kindness and with mercy. 'The sabbath was theirs—the court of the Gentiles was theirs', the way of access to all the benefits, temporal and spiritual, of the Jewish religion was theirs. They were to be treated with uniform justice and tenderness; as proselytes and converts, in all respects as brethren.

Other Anti-Slavery Ideologues made the same point. Benjamin Godwin showed that the Hebrews were under special dispensation, while Dr Andrew Thomson acknowledged that the ancient Jews had slavery because 'permission was given by Him who is the great proprietor of all . . .'. Slaveholders today, Thomson continued, could not produce such a 'warrant for making property of their black brethren, and reducing them to the condition of slaves'. The Israelites under the authority of God went forth to slay the Canaanites. England too could be justified in destroying any nation if she had the authority of God.

An important Scottish theologian, Ralph Wardlaw, compared ancient Hebrew slavery with the West Indian variety. Like Thomson and Godwin, Wardlaw pointed out that liberty was the 'natural birthright of every man' and only direct divine permission could change this situation. British colonial slavery was based on the 'cupidity of power'. Israelite slavery had 'many alleviating features'. The slaves could participate in the Commonwealth of Israel, could receive religious instruction, and were owned by benevolent masters. If a fellow Hebrew was sold into slavery he was freed after six years and given provisions for future subsistence and well being. The sixth year was the Jubilee Year; and slaves were free on the day of atonement.[31]

Wilberforce had used the same argument to defend African slavery. When critics of the abolitionists answered their attack on slavery by pointing to the fact that there was already slavery in Africa, Wilberforce pointed to the differences between the two systems. In Africa, slaves were often part of the masters' families and had the same rights as other members of the household. There was a filial relationship between master and slave, and the slave had judicial rights of his own. They had a greater right to their persons, for unlike the British slaves they could not be sold except for crimes.

The slave society in the British colonies allowed for little if any individual self expression. It stifled the African's hopes of cultivating an inner spiritual relationship with God. There was no justice for him nor was there any paternal guidance from those that ruled over him. In ancient Israel and in Africa the evidence pointed to a contrary state of affairs. Hence that kind of slavery was not open to the same kind of indictment as the slave society in the British colonies.

Thus from a theoretical point of view, abolitionists did not condemn all kinds of slavery. The slaves of the ancient Israelites could have their religion and were freed after a given number of years. This form of slavery was not severe nor did it prevent those that were enslaved from having their own God. And their servitude was not for life nor was it perpetuated over the generations. Thus they were not deprived of their right to individual self-expression and spiritual identity by their servitude. Though the property of others, they had rights of their own.

The impact that these arguments had on the public helped to create a greater and greater demand for immediate emancipation. Not only were the British people lectured on the evils of the slave society but their sense of conscience and guilt was also exploited in still another Anti-Slavery argument. The theme of retribution—that dire consequences would befall the nation and her people should emancipation

[31] George Thompson, *An Address To The Ladies of Glasgow and Vicinity On Negro Emancipation*, 5 March, 1833 (Glasgow, 1833), p. 11. Andrew Thomson, *Immediate Emancipation*, p. 17. Ralph Wardlaw, *The Jubilee Sermon*, 1 August 1834 (Glasgow, 1834), p. 6.

not be brought about—was commonly preached before Anti-Slavery audiences. As in other areas of Anti-Slavery thought, the new rationalizations for emancipation were stamped with evangelical characteristics.

The imminent fear of retribution fitted in easily and conveniently with the new priorities and that new sense of an urgent drive for a final solution. In earlier periods this preoccupation with retribution had expressed itself in goals of reform. After 1830 it could mean one thing only—emancipation. In terms of the movement's ideological outlook, however, there was little difference between the earlier and later pronouncements.

The evangelicals within the Church of England were like their colleagues of dissenting faiths adamant on this point. In 1807 Wilberforce addressed his constitutents in Yorkshire on the abolition of the slave trade. It was a 'national crime . . . a crime to which we cling in defiance of the clearest light, not only in opposition to our own acknowledgement of its guilt, but even of our declared resolutions to abandon it'. The nation therefore should strenuously endeavour 'to lighten the vessel of the state, of such a load of guilt and infamy'. As individuals could feel guilt when they sinned, so abolitionist crusaders attributed the same feelings to their own nation. Wilberforce believed that the trade was 'the foulest blot that ever stained our national character', and prided himself on 'having been among the foremost in wiping it away'.

Thomas Clarkson also dwelt on the idea of national guilt as a result of Britain's support of the slave trade. At the end of his two-volume treatise on the abolitionist movement he proclaimed that 'the stain of the blood of Africa is no longer upon us', and that England had been freed 'from a load of guilt, which has long hung like a millstone about our necks, ready to sink us to perdition'. Clarkson dominated the abolitionist movement and was driven by a sense of mission to purify not only individuals but the nation as a whole. This was a moral nationalism. Clarkson declared that as a result of the abolition of the trade 'we have lived . . . to see the day, when it has been recorded as a principle in our legislation, that commerce itself shall have its moral boundaries'.[32]

Not only the slave had to be delivered from the evil but the nation as a whole must be cleansed of the guilt that support of the system had created. Earlier, abolition of the slave trade had been the cry to save the nation. In 1832 it was emancipation and that alone that would purge Great Britain and its people of that guilt. George Thompson, speaking before the Glasgow Ladies' Emancipation Society in 1833 declared:

[32] Wilberforce, *A Letter*, pp. 5–6, 91–2, 107. Clarkson, *History*, vol. II, pp. 583–4.

If for these things the judgment of God should come upon us, we cannot say we have not been warned. Rolling thunders and sweeping hurricanes, and wild tornadoes, and desolating earthquakes, and raging fevers, and declining commerce, and a dying population, and weeping mercy, and insulted justice, and reason, and religion, and God, have said again and again, 'Let these people go'. Their voices are still heard; let us, though late, obey. (Doc. 6)

Joseph Ivimey, a Baptist minister speaking for the Agency Committee, saw in the course of events the possibility of total destruction. Citing the biblical example of Nineveh and Tyre as Granville Sharp had done before him, Ivimey noted that God had destroyed them because they traded in men. Ivimey admonished, 'O England thou modern Tyre in wealth, in crime especially by the merchants—Repent.' The Bible, Ivimey pointed out, had predicted that these cities would fall. Looking at the contemporary course of events, Ivimey believed that there were signs of coming catastrophes for England too. There were 'infalliable signs' that preceded 'the Lord's destruction of Jerusalem'. He enumerated the present signs that might lead to chaos. There was a hurricane in Barbados and the 'awful insurrection in Jamaica'. The 'indescribable wickedness and profaneness that prevail among its inhabitants especially the whites' was punished through the insurrection. Ivimey would not be 'surprised' if 'the hand of God had gone out against them'. Further Jamaica's 'implacable malice shown towards the Baptist Missionaries' may cause the island's downfall as Jerusalem had fallen.[33]

It was common practice for the Anti-Slavery Society to combine the most sophisticated of instructions concerning strategy and tactics with prophesies of retribution and doom should the instructions not be followed. Worldly means used to create spiritual ends was the common vision of English abolitionists. They believed that this was as it should be, a part of the providential plan of the whole universe.

England could reform and relieve herself of her guilt only if she accomplished a positive good in the colonies. The future religious life of the slave as a man of God was as much at stake as that of the present religious life of every God-fearing Christian. There was an inexonerable link between the religious vitality of the English nation and that of the slave.

In this sense the theme of retribution had a positive side as well. For it then became the nation's imperative mission to prevent retribution by demonstrating to the rest of the world that it had a moral backbone.

[33] Thompson, *An Address*, p. 30. Joseph Ivimey, *The Utter Extinction of Slavery* (London, 1832), pp. 32, 40, 44.

A sense of national pride and purpose; a righteous self-image would then be created. Great Britain by abolishing slavery would be the Christian example for the international community. In 1833 a congregationalist advocate of emancipation, Robert Halley, proclaimed that if slavery was abolished the 'great national reproach will be rolled away and Britain become an example to the world of the strength of religious principle nobly triumphing over the avarice and heartlessness of commercial speculation'.

Still another aspect of the abolitionist appeal to British nationalism concerned the traditions of freedom which enabled the British nation successfully to resist tyranny in Europe. 'With what a feeling of generous pride did every bosom swell when England was hailed as the liberator of Europe!' commented Godwin. Yet 'she sends her armies and her fleets to the West Indies to rivet the chains of slavery on her own subjects . . .'. Great Britain had been a success in the Napoleonic Wars and had expended great efforts to defeat oligarchic might, and yet she gladly tolerated this in her own colonies. And what was still more damnable was that both her Christian tradition and her political traditions were being violated at the same time. Slavery had to be abolished to preserve the character of the nation: that image of a Christian, liberty-loving nation. Then she should 'rank high among the nations'. Great Britain could continue to play a role in the international community as the champion of liberty if she would abolish slavery immediately. Otherwise she would lose her first-ranking position in the world and be 'compelled to take a mortifying position, in the rear of those of whom she had always been in advance'. Great Britain's national power and glory, the great place she had created for herself among the nations of the world would all be wiped away. If she should fail to maintain her reputation then every aspect of British national might and power could be destroyed. The British nation's commitment to Christian liberty had created its great national strength and she must uphold this commitment.[34]

The ideological concerns of the Anti-Slavery Movement were clearly delineated along the lines of religious morality. Both leaders and followers were dedicated to saving the souls of men. Thus it is a misnomer to characterize the movement as humanitarian. Its narrow orthodoxy left little room for concern with the plight of any other portions of suffering humanity. They were free men and were not hindered from finding religion. Thus the Dissenters did not all share an equal enthusiasm for the plight of the working class. Many indus-

[34] Robert Halley, *The Sinfulness of Colonial Slavery: Lecture*, 7 February 1833 (London, 1833), p. 27. Godwin, *Lectures*, pp. 160, 252–5.

trialists were members of dissenting churches and it was their ministers who condemned efforts of Tory evangelicals to secure better conditions for workers. They openly condemned the Factory Acts. Richard Oastler complained that their rigid piety was no help when it came to the treatment of their own workers.

Major portions of Methodist and Baptist theology advocated an acceptance of the status quo of society as a means of maintaining the security of the social order. Nonconformists of whatever denomination failed to take decisive positions on any of the great social questions relating to the industrial revolution. They remained either ambivalent or divided over the major problems of social change. Throughout the nineteenth century, beginning with the Anti-Slavery agitation, they concentrated their efforts as denominational groups on moral questions.[35]

It was the Tory aristocrats rather than the Anti-Slavery Movement with its following of Dissenters that demonstrated humanitarian concern at home. In 1832 Thomas Sadler, a Tory evangelical from Leeds, introduced into parliament the first measure for the reform of working conditions in the manufacturing districts. Clearly his stand was not to the liking of his constituents who cast their votes for the first time under the Reform Act of 1832. For the most part Dissenters, they routed Sadler out of office and supported Thomas Babington Macaulay whose loyalty to the Anti-Slavery cause was so well known.

That dissenting preoccupation with morality was hardly humanitarian was demonstrated by the fate of the first Factory Act. Lord Morpeth, another MP from that Dissenter stronghold, Yorkshire (West Riding), tried to dilute the measures for factory reform that did finally pass the first reform parliament. The measure that was enacted in the parliament that passed the act to emancipate the slaves was a weak and ineffectual one. It failed to regulate most of the major abuses of the industrial system. Thus the strong political backing that the Anti-Slavery Movement had in 1833 and the constituents it represented saw little need to be humanitarian, though they felt urgently compelled to be moralistic.[36]

The Anti-Slavery Movement's narrow focus on morality provided a framework for the ideological gathering of Protestant communities.

[35] The 'humanitarian' label has been applied most notably by Reginald Coupland, *The British Anti-Slavery Movement* (London, 1933), Frank J. Klingberg, *The Anti-Slavery Movement in England: A Study in English Humanitarianism* (New Haven, 1926), and G. R. Mellor, *British Imperial Trusteeship 1783–1850* (London, 1951).

[36] C. M. Elliot, 'The Political Economy of English Dissent 1780–1840', R. M. Hartwell, editor, *The Industrial Revolution* (Oxford, 1970), pp. 157, 166. Elie Halévy, *The Liberal Awakening* (London, 1949), pp. 110–11.

Anti-Slavery thought cannot be divorced from the general body of Protestant theology. Its textures were woven by deeply committed Christian minds that shared a Christian world-view of events. They defined life in terms of a doctrine which supported this view. Because Protestant thought had its genesis in a doctrinal protest which led to theological revisions, Protestants thereafter sought to justify all behaviour in terms of doctrine. Religion was doctrine and doctrine was life.

Anti-Slavery thought was but one of several definitions of doctrine available to British Protestants in the late eighteenth and nineteenth centuries. Its particular vitality and attractive dynamic took hold of the Protestant mind. Christianity declares that God reveals himself in history and makes himself known to a given group of men in a given society. The Anti-Slavery argument allowed for a revealed God who would make himself known not only to those already in possession of his revelation but to those who would seek his revelation. Thus it was the omnipotent available God which would be worshipped by all men which would be rejected by the slave society. Its leaders did not allow their slaves to find the God of history as revealed in living thoughts in the Bible. Hence Protestant self-definition was threatened in its most fundamental ideological terms.

In the notion of a collective consciousness there is the thought that intention carries weight even if it is not fulfilled. When the British nation supported the slave society then, the logical corollary was that her intention was evil. Her Christian communities began to question this and having good intentions they found the spiritual dedication to change the evil ways of their nation. The Protestant follows his calling in a community setting where the faithful participates in the life, witness and charitable action of the community. True believers are thus easily identifiable as they demonstrate through acts within the group their loyalty to God.[37]

Anti-Slavery societies and Anti-Slavery meetings followed the Protestant congregationalist communities' organizational pattern. Every individual had his personal commitment, his society and his local church. Thus the patterning for petitioning in parliament in 1831–3 for the abolition of slavery was by denomination in a given local community. Membership in the Anti-Slavery Society's local branches enhanced an already deep and rich commitment to religious faith. Hence it was with the first and most fundamental unit of organization, the denominational congregation, that the people wished to identify their protests.

Protestantism consists both in acts and in attitudes. They are often

[37] For a sociological interpretation of Protestantism see Roger Mehl, *The Sociology of Protestantism* (London, 1970), *passim*.

unforeseeable and non-codifiable demonstrations of piety and faith. Acts are not conditions of salvation but the consequences of salvation. To be committed to the Anti-Slavery ideology would be such an act. The mystery of the unknown and all powerful God became better known through acts of commitment and faith.

These acts through the centuries created the Protestant tradition. By engrafting tradition upon tradition, the Protestant community makes that tradition more authoritative. By engrafting tradition upon tradition, the Protestant community attempts to breathe a new authority into it. Central to Christian tradition is the notion of the mystery of God which can be interpreted and explained in a variety of ways; it is a history of experiences of Christians which make more explicit the mystery of faith; a faith that is both tangible and intangible, a faith which by the very nature of the ambiguity of the unknown God needs constant redefinition. In essence Protestant ideology is a confession of faith having its roots in revelation and conversion. The ideal of an ecclesiology of the Protestant type would be to consider each member as exercising a particular ministry in the Church, creating his own tradition. Thus the dedication and devotion needed to fight for reformist goals are present in the fundamental commitment of the believer. He feels no alienation or rejection in his participation. Rather he finds in it a logical outcome and a needed corollary for the demonstration of his faith. Hence the characteristic and unremitting devotion of the leaders and followers of the Anti-Slavery movement.

The aims, techniques and goals of social reform movements fit neatly into the mould of Protestant thought. Protestant societies are most concerned with proclaiming a truth, gathering about a message, and assuring a spiritual communion. These practices are inseparable from the life of the community. The great emphasis that the movement's ideology places on written proof for its attack on slavery ties in neatly too with the reliance that Protestantism places on the sources of revelation found in the Bible. As God's revelation could be proved by the Bible, so the Almighty's indictment of the slave society could be substantiated by written proof. The biblical pronouncements concerning ancient societies and the causes of their wickedness then became examples of what could happen to British colonial slave society. Thus Nineveh and Tyre were frequently cited in the tracts as cities that had suffered retribution because they had not followed the revealed teachings of the Lord.

There was great comfort in objectifying God's spirit through an endless flow of words. The torment, the anxiety of the unknown would be somewhat eased. The finite and infinite meshed. Hence the Protestant savoured God's meaning as revelation. Words for the Christian carried the power of transcendence. The Protestant, longing for this, tasted it in speech and prayer. He objectified it and made it tangible in the printed word. In assembly with others he coped with its mystery and the intangibles connected with God's powers. Retribution, the opposite of transcendence, was also an imminent possibility. Hence the thousands upon thousands of words both written and spoken to balance the emotional striving for transcendence and to relieve the fear of retribution.

As a cultural ideal, God is dead and does not now dominate the universe as he reigned in the nineteenth century. Instead all aspects of life today—be it in the past, present or future—are dominated by the notion of time. It is the dictates of time rather than the requisites of transcendence through spirit that dominate the western world. Emotional energy is spent in great amounts worrying about time, and there is no hope of uplift or support. Instead there is the ever present drive to use time, and for instantaneous gratification. Modern man is, in his immediate world, limited by *time*: and the dictates of that fleeting, precious and often illusive phenomenon.

Modern man dominated by time does not find in his surrender the transcendence that the nineteenth-century evangelical felt in his surrender to God. Western culture is dominated by words that proclaim love and hence promise transcendence. Yet they offer little comfort for alienated, lonely humanity who find that words only promise something that as members of society, as a part of a community, they do not feel. If words are any comfort at all it is like time itself a momentary and fleeting experience.

Without the hope of salvation, modern man can never quite fathom nor fully appreciate the comfort that words might have had for the nineteenth-century evangelical, no matter how profusely he uses them. Thus to the contemporary mind the abundance of literature of all kinds—tracts, books, magazines, petitions, posters—that came out of the Anti-Slavery Movement as ideology would seem repetitious in its content, redundant in its meaning. Yet, for the British evangelical of the nineteenth century, there could never be enough exhortation or repetition of truths that were infused with emotional uplift.

The abolitionist ideology strengthened the security of the individual. The movement provided a forum for Protestants to express and turn to positive focus their experience as believers. Social reform movements of the abolitionist variety successfully bridged the gap between the society and the religious universe by creating an alliance of authentic Christian witness in the presence of the secularized world.

'Will,' R. H. Tawney has noted, 'is the essence of Puritanism, and for the intensification and organization of will every instrument in that tremendous arsenal of religious fervor is mobilized.' The crushing impact that the movement had on nineteenth-century England suggests that it harnessed the Puritain 'will' in a manner never to be repeated. The Puritan, Tawney concluded, 'is like a spring compressed by an inner force, which shatters every obstacle by its rebound'. The Anti-Slavery Movement moulded that inner, explodable tension so that the collective will shattered every obstacle in the path of reform. Its ideology triumphed because it warded off fears of a revengeful God and instead bestowed confidence on the uneasy Protestant conscience.[38]

[38] *Religion and the Rise of Capitalism*, p. 201. The characteristics of Protestant belief systems and society as compared to Catholic belief systems and society are discussed by Richard M. Morse, *Comments on Slavery in the United States and Brazil*, a paper presented at the sixty-second annual meeting of the organization of American historians (Philadelphia, 17 April 1969).

3

Politics and the Public Conscience: the Anti-Slavery Movement and the Emancipation Act, 1831–40

Whig leaders were from the aristocratic class that had created the patriarchal tradition. Political office had always been available to aristocrats and they had prided themselves on their responsible use of power. They sought to fulfil their obligations by demonstrating their respect for the issues which the middle class felt strongly about. It was the Whig government which came to power in 1830 and fought for the representation of portions of the middle class in parliament when it sponsored the Reform Bill of 1832. A year later that same Whig cabinet would commit itself to the abolition of slavery—another cause that had strong middle-class support. The patriarchal tradition of the British aristocracy lived on in the early 1830s in the response of the Whigs to the demands of the British middle class.[1]

The Whig prime minister, Earl Grey, instructed the Committee of Four, which drafted the first version of the Reform Bill, to 'satisfy all reasonable demands, and remove once and forever, all rational grounds for complaint from the minds of the intelligent and independent portion of the community'. The 'intelligent and independent' were from the middle class, many of them followers of dissenting religions and very much opposed to slavery. The Reform Bill, it was hoped, would bring these groups under the wing of the establishment lest they stray to more radical alternatives.[2]

[1] For a general discussion of the patriarchal tradition in English history, cf. Harold Perkin, *The Origins of Modern English Society (1780–1880)* (London, 1969), *passim*. Aristocrats, sensitive to public opinion, are discussed in W. L. Guttsman, *British Political Elites* (London, 1964). A detailed analysis of the Whig leadership during the reform crises can be found in Allan Silver, 'Social and Ideological Bases of the British Elite's Reactions to Domestic Crises, 1829–1832', *Politics and Society*, vol. I (February, 1971), pp. 181–93.

[2] Asa Briggs, *The Age of Improvement* (London, 1954), pp. 237–40. Donald

Anti-Slavery leaders in parliament were quick to recognize that the fate of the emancipation issue was inextricably tied to parliamentary reform. The dynamic state of political affairs in the nation must be made use of, they knew, to win additional supporters in parliament for the abolition of slavery. At the annual meeting of the society held in Exeter Hall in London just prior to the election of April 1831 the membership unanimously approved a resolution calling for the immediate abolition of colonial slavery. Members were instructed to return to their localities and to make emancipation an issue of the forthcoming election. Committees were to be formed in each district and were given the responsibility of making strict inquiries of every candidate 'not only whether he is decidedly favourable to the extinction of slavery, but whether or not he will attend the Debates in Parliament when the question is discussed. . .'[3]

Recognizing that social change was not only in the air but being blown in on powerful winds, abolitionists sought to utilize the new currents circulating everywhere to their own advantage. The political task before them was far greater than anything ever undertaken by the Anti-Slavery Movement. To meet the formidable challenge a new group emerged from the membership which called itself the Agency Committee. Its purpose was to recruit organizers who would tour the country to promote public discussions that would make new converts to the abolitionist cause. Many new branches of the society would also be formed as a result of these visits.

The founders of the Agency Committee noted the success which the strategy and tactics of the political unions had achieved in bringing about national support for the reform of parliament. The appeal had been from the countryside, local organizations in the boroughs and in the provinces. The Agency Committee sought to marshal these same forces to exert political pressure on the government to bring about emancipation.[4]

Southgate, *The Passing of the Whigs* (London, 1962), p. 22. Joseph Hamburger, *Intellectuals in Politics: John Stuart Mill and the Philosophical Radicals* (New Haven, 1963). The 1830 revolution in France made the Whigs fearful of revolt at home should demands be ignored. Concession was required instead, ibid., p. 35. For an account of the passing of the Reform Bill see J. R. M. Butler, *The Passing of the Great Reform Bill* (London, 1914).

[3] *Anti-Slavery Reporter*, vol. 4 (May 1831), pp. 140–5, for report of meeting. The Society also issued an *Address to the People of Great Britain and Ireland* (London, 1831), setting forth the reasons for its policy and including the resolutions adopted at its annual meeting in Exeter Hall on 23 April 1831.

[4] For the formation of the Agency Committee cf. George Stephen, *Anti-Slavery Recollections* (London, 1859), pp. 127–35. Still an earlier precedent for

While the Agency Committee did nothing to discredit the traditional leadership of the parent society, they employed novel methods to achieve their aims. The membership of the London Committee (which made general policy for the movement) was drawn for the most part from members of parliament and evangelical anglicans who were usually cautious and conservative. Presenting petitions and promoting the issue in government circles was their course of action. Whereas they had relied on the use of printed literature and directives to rally the local societies in the provinces, the Agency Committee sent agitators to go directly to the localities to organize new societies and to increase the membership of the older ones. Its proposals did not meet with the immediate approval of the London Committee. However, on the national level its methods won the endorsement of the entire membership.[5]

The Agency Committee sought to implement its programme without subjecting it to the approval of the London Committee of the Anti-Slavery Society. Dissenters played important roles in its operations, and their participation was fundamental to its success. George Stephen admitted that Emanuel and Joseph Cooper (both Quakers) were two of the three 'working men' of the committee. Still another member of the Society of Friends, James Cropper, provided significant financial support. Three of its most effective, inspiring and popular stipendiary agents—George Thompson, Joseph Ivimey and William Knibb—were Methodist and Baptists respectively.

It was apparent that the question of emancipation was as vital a subject in the countryside as the fate of the Reform Bill itself. There were enthusiastic receptions given to the speakers wherever they turned, and agents reported that many 'conversions' were made.

---

interest group pressure politics on the provincial level was Daniel O'Connell's Catholic Association and New Catholic Association. In 1826, they had secured MP support for Catholic emancipation in the localities. R. K. Webb, *Modern England* (London, 1969; New York, 1970), pp. 188–9 and Elie Halévy, *The Liberal Awakening* (London, 1949), p. 222.

[5] George Stephen, *Anti-Slavery Recollections*, 128. David Brion Davis, 'James Cropper and the British Anti-Slavery Movement,' *Journal of Negro History*, vol. 46 (1961), p. 167. Perhaps it was the new tactics of Committee rather than a difference of opinion as to the goals of emancipation which led Stephen to characterize the Agency founders as 'Young English Abolitionists'. For still another account of the founding of the Agency Committee, cf. (ed.) Henry Richard, *Memoirs of Joseph Sturge* (London, 1865), p. 94. After the formation of the Agency Committee, the number of affiliated societies rose from 200 to 1,300. Reginald Coupland, *The British Anti-Slavery Movement* (London, 1933), p. 137.

Writing to the committee from the town of Olney, an agent reported that:

> I was quite amazed to see the interest which our cause excites, seeing the intensity of feeling of the fate of the reform bill. Though under great temptation, I am strictly obedient to my instructions not to mingle politics with my advocacy of Negro freedom, and yet I observe an ardour equal to political enthusiasm'.[6]

By 1832, leaders were further radicalized as a result of the appointment of eight slave owners to the select committee of the Lords to investigate slavery. 'They had asked for the extinction of slavery,' Buxton remarked indignantly to the enthusiastic audience, 'and had gotten a Committee of Lords.' Buxton told his followers that in the past year the 'advocates of the Negro have met with opposition and desertion'.[7]

Anxiety concerning the outcome of their cause had always been characteristic of the membership of the Anti-Slavery Movement. It would appear that the formation of the Agency Committee was an expression of that anxiety, coming as it did at a time of great political chaos in the nation. George Stephen, one of its founders, recalled the fear he felt at the time. He was sure that the agitation related to the Reform Bill had left the nation as a whole with little political energy or interest for any other cause. It had created a 'lull behind', leaving Anti-Slavery opinion in 'suspended animation'. Lest the people think only of reform of parliament and not in the colonies, the opportunity must be seized and utilized to the best advantage. Nothing could be taken for granted even though Buxton, on 29 March 1831, had presented 499 petitions for emancipation to the House.

Stephen recalled that 'it was a subject of frequent and anxious consideration' of how to keep the cause as a popular issue before the public. And indeed there was something to be anxious about, for the Whig government took no decisive stand on the emancipation issue. Buxton's parliamentary speech on slave mortality of 15 April 1831 which documented the steady decline of the slave population in the colonies failed to convince the Whigs to change government policy. On 27 June 1831, the undersecretary of state for the colonies, Viscount

---

[6] *Report of the Agency Committee of the Anti-Slavery Society Established June, 1831* (London, 1832), p. 11 (see Doc. 4). George Stephen, *Anti-Slavery Recollections*, pp. 132, 147–9. Davis, *J.N.H.*, vol. 46, p. 169.

[7] Quoted in *Anti-Slavery Reporter*, vol. 5 (May 1832), p. 144. It was common gossip that the Archbishop of Canterbury had forced the government to appoint the Committee. It was understood that if the Committee was appointed, his support for the Reform Bill would be assured. *Christian Observer*, vol. 32 (June 1832), p. 368.

Howick, announced in parliament that ministers would offer no new proposals for freeing the slaves in the colonies. His father, Prime Minister Earl Grey, was indifferent personally to the entire matter. Howick had denounced slavery in a speech in the House of Commons. When Thomas F. Buxton praised his attitude, Grey remarked that his son was too zealous in his beliefs.[8]

The desertion of the government was all the more disastrous because of the events in Jamaica. A slave rebellion there had been followed by a reign of lawlessness; missionaries of dissenting faiths in the colony had been jailed and persecuted. The indifference of the Whig government to the terror made Buxton even more determined to press for emancipation. Though the government had just passed through a political crisis and the second Whig cabinet of May, formed on the 15th, was but a week old, Buxton advised them that he would bring forward a motion in parliament for the abolition of slavery. Whig ministers (Howick and Althorp) warned that it was not expedient to make emancipation a political issue when the question of reform was still to be settled. Buxton decided to run the risk of alienating his Whig allies and even his closest political friends. Propelled by a sense of great moral urgency, he was committed to standing alone. Believing that the missionaries and the slaves had suffered far more already than he ever could, he felt bound to alleviate their suffering. Doing away with slavery was the only real solution possible.

On 24 May 1832, Buxton proposed in parliament that a select committee should be appointed 'for the purpose of effecting the extinction of slavery throughout the British dominions at the earliest period compatible with the safety of all classes in the colonies'. The popularity of the issue had already changed the views of Whigs. Before 24 May Lord Althorp had opposed Buxton, but now he sought only to modify the proposal. He amended it so that the motion should take into account the 'interests' as well as the safety of all classes and then that it should be extended by the words 'and in conformity with the resolutions of the House of 15 May 1823'. Buxton though pressured by many fellow MPs to agree to this modification stood behind his original motion (which was lost by a small majority).

Buxton told his friends that the cause had made a 'seven league stride'. On 6 June 1832 a committee of the House of Commons was appointed to determine the grounds for the abolition of slavery. Buxton's optimism was truly justified.[9]

[8] *Memoirs of Sir Thomas F. Buxton*, pp. 244–5.
[9] Ibid., pp. 246, 249. William L. Mathieson, *British Slavery and Its Abolition* (London, 1926), pp. 223–4 (see Doc. 3).

Anti-Slavery forces had failed to secure a definitive commitment from the government during the summer of 1832. There were, however, discussions in government circles and in the committee meetings in parliament. But official policy remained based on the Order in Council of 2 November 1831 that proposed ameliorative measures for the slaves in line with the parliamentary resolutions of 1823. It was issued in the hope that co-operation from Jamaica and the other colonies would put off abolitionist pressure for immediate emancipation. Viscount Goderich, the secretary of state for the colonies, hoped that the slaves would be able, in their spare time, to earn enough money to buy their own freedom. He believed this procedure might be accepted as a settlement of the question.[10]

The emancipation issue was brought before the public with even greater power when the persecuted missionaries returned from Jamaica in September 1832. They reported that chapels were destroyed and missionaries were tried for allegedly working with the rebels. They were then exiled to England. Slurs in the local press against them were common. 'Ruffians, preaching miscreants and vagabonding reverends' were common labels. The most vicious result of the fear, tension and mistrust which took hold of the white population was the formation of the Colonial Church Union. This Jamaican equivalent of the Vigilantes rode through the countryside burning Methodist and Baptist chapels as well as missionary homes. A value of £25,000 was placed on the damage done. An abortive attempt was made to convict the missionaries of treason.

When William Knibb, the most celebrated of the Jamaican missionaries, returned to England and was told that the Reform Bill had passed, he is reported to have exclaimed, 'Thank God, now I'll have slavery down'.[11] Knibb toured the countryside carrying his plea for emancipation to Bristol, Birmingham, Liverpool, Manchester, Norwich,

---

[10] For an account of the reaction of the Jamaica Assembly to these proposals see Samuel J. and Edith F. Hurwitz, *Jamaica: A Historical Portrait* (London, 1972; New York, 1971), pp. 87–120. Goderich's views are presented by Wilbur D. Jones, *Prosperity Robinson* (New York, 1967), p. 223. On 9 June 1832, Goderich sent a circular dispatch to the colonial governors with the new offer. Cf. Vincent Harlow and Frederick Madden, *British Colonial Documents, 1774–1834* (Oxford, 1953), p. 587.

[11] Quoted in Henry Richard, *Sturge*, p. 100. For events in Jamaica, see Samuel J. and Edith F. Hurwitz, *Jamaica*, pp. 113–18 and the accounts of other missionaries who were there. Henry Bleby, *Death Struggles in Slavery* (London, 1853); John Howard Hinton, *Memoirs of William Knibb* (London, 1847); and Mary Reckford, 'The Jamaica Slave Rebellion of 1831', *Past and Present*, vol. 16 (July 1968), pp. 109–25.

Reading, Glasgow and Edinburgh. He called on the ministers of religion to speak out against the evil. Thus an important group of Dissenters, the Wesleyan Methodists, in July 1832 were committed to immediate emancipation. Knibb was an important and convincing witness before both the House of Commons and House of Lords committees on slavery in 1832 and had a talk with Howick that converted him to emancipation. His declaration before an audience in Scotland that 'I have come to dig the grave of colonial slavery, to entomb the greatest curse that ever rested on Britain' was to become a self-fulfilling prophecy.[12]

On 27 September 1832 the London Committee of the Anti-Slavery Society advised all members to be aware of the links between the emancipation question and the general election. The Committee warned its members not to promise your 'suffrages to any candidate until they will support total emancipation'. The radical and conservative elements of the Anti-Slavery Movement had come to terms for the first time. By the end of 1832 the London Committee was contributing funds to the Agency Commitee. They had broken apart in July of 1832, but the new moral urgency had reunited them in the autumn.[13]

The Agency Committee stepped up its activities on several fronts. A plan was devised for reaching all parts of the kingdom. The number of stipendiary agents was increased. Several dissenting ministers volunteered to help. England was divided into districts for the agents to cover. The western and southern sections of the country were given first consideration. Seven national routes were worked out in all. Under the terms of the Reform Act the agricultural south continued to be over-represented in parliament. Hence the Committee's concentration of forces there. In all 345,000 English county voters controlled 114 seats while 275,000 borough voters controlled 327 seats.[14] The Anti-Slavery Society had succeeded in making a public issue of emancipation. The impact on candidates for office was considerable. A sampling of the

---

[12] John Howard Hinton, *Memoirs of William Knibb*, p. 157. It was at this point that Viscount Howick and Undersecretaries Henry Taylor and James Stephen of the colonial office began to draw up definitive proposals for emancipation. D. J. Murray, *The West Indies and the Development of Colonial Government* (London, 1965), p. 165.

[13] *Anti-Slavery Reporter*, vol. 5 (24 September 1832), p. 292. The new unity is also discussed by D. Eltis, 'Dr Stephen Lushington and the Campaign to Abolish Slavery in the British Empire,' *Journal of Caribbean History*, vol. I (November 1970), p. 49, and by Davis, *J.N.H.*, vol. 46, pp. 167–9 (see Doc. 5).

[14] Asa Briggs, *The Age of Improvement*, pp. 261–2. Public debates between agents of the Committee and agents of the West Indian interest were common. Agents of the Agency Committee almost invariably won. George Stephen, *Anti-Slavery Recollections*, pp. 153–5.

electoral contests in 1832 shows that it was not the industrial north aligned against the agricultural south, or the newly enfranchised boroughs versus the older counties and pocket boroughs that determined the nature of Anti-Slavery opinion and commitment to immediate emancipation. The high principles, the immutable truths of the religious appeal penetrated into boroughs and counties of all sizes and in both the north and the south.[15]

Sheffield, a borough that had, as a result of the Reform Bill, sent its own delegates to parliament for the first time, was solidly Anti-Slavery. Before the Act it had been a part of the West Riding of Yorkshire. Now its candidates—four in all—were forced to declare themselves ardent supporters of emancipation. They took prominent parts in the lectures of the Anti-Slavery Society. Though there had been some semblance of an Anti-Slavery Society in Sheffield before 1825, it was only after one of the stipendiary agents of the Committee lectured there in July 1832 that a militant, vigilant organization was formed under the chairmanship of the prominent local reformer, poet and journalist, James Montgomery.[16] In the course of the debates on the Emancipation Act, one of its two MPs would side with Buxton's most radical amendments.

But if Sheffield was a solid stronghold of the cause, what about the 'pocket borough' of Buckingham that survived the reform of parliament unchanged? There must have been less than three hundred voters casting their ballots in the first reform election. Candidates for office had long needed the support of the borough's principal landowner, the Duke of Buckingham. In 1831 candidates running for office in the April election refrained from declaring their preferences on all issues except that of colonial slavery. One candidate, though he had been known to be associated with the West India interest, had advocated gradual emancipation in 1831. During the December 1832 election he was defeated.

In Buckingham the candidates who took a stand for immediate emancipation easily won the first election under the first reform act. Sir Harry Verney, a devout evangelist who had the support of the Dissenters and the Quakers, polled the greatest number of votes in the

[15] The Agency Committee was no doubt influenced by the tactics of political radicals. Frances Place had compiled a list of candidates who were for or against reform during the 1831 election. The National Political Union came out in support of the abolition of slavery in July 1832. Graham Wallace, *Frances Place* (London, 1925), pp. 262, 327.

[16] N. B. Lewis, 'The Abolition Movement in Sheffield, 1823–1833, with Letters from Southey, Wordsworth and Others,' *John Rylands Library Bulletin*, vol. 17 (1933), p. 380.

borough. He was clearly not the Duke's candidate who ran third and lost. The Duke's ironmonger was secretary of the Buckingham Anti-Slavery Society, and thirty-three of the voters who were dependent on the Duke for a living voted for Verney and thirty-three others for Freemantle, the other avowed Anti-Slavery candidate. High principle won out over privilege and interest for the Duke strongly desired that Verney be defeated.[17] Buckingham's MPs would, in the course of the debate on the stipulations of the Emancipation Act, take the side of the most radical abolitionist demands.

In the West Riding of Yorkshire, where abolitionist strength had already showed itself in the 1830 election, 'feelings were high', wrote Lord Morpeth to Lord Althorp on 26 December 1832. George Strickland, MP from that area, later commented that he could not have secured a single vote there unless he had already had a reputation as an abolitionist. Political observers knew that what happened in Yorkshire, the largest constituency in England, was a significant indication of how the rest of the country would act. Strickland and the West Riding's other MP, Lord Morpeth, would, throughout the parliamentary debates on the emancipation issue, side with the most radical advocates of emancipation. Still another MP from East Yorkshire, P.E. Thompson, was a deeply committed emancipationist.[18]

Berkshire, an agricultural county in the south, felt little of the strains of the industrial revolution, yet it had constituents who demanded strong commitment on the part of its representatives to the emancipation of the slaves. Its county capital, Reading, was solidly prosperous and middle class. It was given an additional representative as a result of the Reform Act. Of Berkshire's nine representatives in parliament, there were at least five who were committed to immediate emancipation. Charles Russell, a conservative candidate who had been uncommitted to emancipation in the 1831 election was forced to change his attitude in 1832. After some deliberation he pronounced in favour of emancipation, provided compensation was given to the planters. Although he was conservative by inclination, as an MP from Reading where Dissenters were numerous and the spirit of reform strong, he had little choice but to conciliate liberal opinion.

In this county of Berkshire, where there were four candidates for three positions, three out of the four were in favour of immediate

[17] R. W. Davis, 'Buckingham, 1832–1846: a Study of a Pocket Borough', *Huntington Library Quarterly*, vol. 34 (February 1971), pp. 163–7.

[18] Denis Le Marchant, *Memoirs of John Charles Althorp, Third Earl Spenser* (London, 1876), p. 448. *Anti-Slavery Reporter*, vol. 6 (April 1833), p. 74. Strickland made those comments at the Anti-Slavery meeting of 2 April 1833.

emancipation. Two of the reformers were elected as compared to one of the conservatives, although people in general voted on issues rather than parties. In speeches on nomination day, which were the final test of a candidate's position, the important topics were church tithes, corn laws and the abolition of slavery. Anti-Slavery opinion was so vehement in Berkshire that in subsequent debates concerning the emancipation act four out of five representatives from Reading and from the county would support the most radical amendments of the Anti-Slavery forces.[19]

From the largest county in the North, Yorkshire, to aristocratic Buckingham and to the agricultural Berkshire in the south the penetration of the Anti-Slavery forces had been extensive and triumphant. After the election of 10 December 1832, many public personages were aware of this as never before. It was the opinion of one Scotsman that, because of the election, the issue 'must be brought under consideration of the reformed parliament in the first session, [of that] no one could doubt who had noted the zeal of the promoters and the hold which it had evidently taken on the public mind'.[20] The King's secretary, C. F. Greville, remarked in his diary early in 1833 that 'of all the political feelings and passions and such, this rage for emancipation is rather more than a consideration of interest—it has always struck me as the most extraordinary and remarkable'.[21] Lord Chancellor Althorp was convinced that 'emancipation would be more popular than the reform bill'![22] Looking back on the results in the spring of 1833, Buxton exclaimed to members of the Society: 'Where was there a contest, north, south, east or west, in which the Anti-Slavery cause did not lead the way' in deciding victory or defeat for a candidate. The answer yes or no to the question 'Are you for the entire and immediate abolition of slavery'? decided the question.[23]

The West India interest as well as the conservative Tory power received a mighty blow as a result of the Reform Act. The boroughs increased their electorate by approximately 50 per cent. These new voters were middle class and loyal to the Whigs. The seats in parliament

[19] Norman Gash, *Politics in the Age of Peel* (London, 1953), pp. 270–322 *passim* and pp. 282–5, 304–5. The first Quaker to be elected to parliament was Joseph Pease.

[20] John Charles Spenser, *The Reform Ministry and the Reform Parliament* (Edinburgh, 1833), p. 7.

[21] Charles C. F. Greville, *A Journal of the Reigns of King George IV and King William IV*, Henry Reeve (ed.) (New York, 1886), vol. II, p. 139.

[22] Lord Broughton, *Recollections of a Long Life*, edited by his daughter Lady Dorchester (London, 1910), vol. III, pp. 268–9.

[23] *Anti-Slavery Reporter*, vol. 6 (1833), p. 60.

for the new boroughs came from the disenfranchisement of rotten boroughs, many of them being Tory strongholds. The unreformed parliament of 1830 had thirty-five representatives of the West India interest; the reformed parliament of 1833 had fourteen.

The alliance of the West India party with the rotten boroughs was well known. Not only political support had been given by the West India interest, but financial support as well. West India representatives had worked with the anti-reform forces in an effort to defeat political change. They were, stated *The Christian Observer*, 'violent admirers of rotten boroughs: they knew, as Lord Wynford has unwarily divulged, that parliamentary reform would abolish Negro slavery'.[24]

Though the abolitionist movement was pleased with its electoral successes, its political strategy was to proceed with caution. T. F. Buxton, the movement's parliamentary spokesman, did not wish to push the Whig government too hard. He knew that abolition must be a cabinet measure and that the Whigs were in a vulnerable position on many issues (Irish coercion, factory regulation). The Reform Act had done little to change the composition or attitude of the House of Lords. It remained solidly Tory. Emancipation, Buxton was sure, could only be promoted by a Whig ministry, and he did not wish to alienate them. Buxton, concluded George Stephen, was placed 'in the most painful relations with all parties'. On one side were the ranks of supporters throughout the nation impatient for victory. On the other was the delicate political situation the Whigs found themselves in. Buxton tried to understand these problems and only took action after carefully considering all alternatives.[25]

King William IV was sensitive to the reactions of the West India body. He had voted against the abolition of the slave trade in 1807 when, as the Duke of Clarence, he was in the House of Lords. Upon the urging of Mr Ellice, a leader of the West India interest, he had taken a decided stand against emancipation. In the course of his speech upon the opening of parliament during the first week in February, he did not once mention nor allude to the emancipation issue. As a result of his negligence, Lord Althorp believed that there was 'great discontent' in the country. Urged by Buxton and Althorp, Grey met with the King. Apparently William IV hoped that the issue would die, for Grey came away from the meeting believing that parliament should not deal with emancipation at all. Soon after, Lord Althorp told Buxton that the

---

[24] *Christian Observer*, vol. 32 (May 1832), p. 367.
[25] George Stephen, *Anti-Slavery Recollections*, pp. 170, 171, 174. *Memoirs of Sir Thomas F. Buxton*, pp. 255–7.

cabinet's real wish was to 'defer it sine die' as 'they were really obliged to do so they were in such a strait'.[26]

The hostility of the King and the Tories and the West India interest notwithstanding, Grey by March was committed to emancipation. Yet the ideas and plans that were before the government were not totally to his liking. Throughout the month of February and most of March a cabinet committee considered the abolitionist plan, the demands of the West Indies and the plan of Viscount Howick, the undersecretary of state for the colonies. Howick was an advocate of compensation in the form of a £15,000,000 loan. Another idea contained in his scheme was that the slaves should be freed by 1835. To insure that the freemen continued to work he proposed that they be placed under the vagrancy laws and that a forty shilling per acre tax should be placed on all food-producing land. This would bind the freemen to the plantations as the tax would have to be paid from their wages.

With all these proposals available, the government delayed in announcing an emancipation plan. Grey had been critical of the pro-abolitionist position of both Goderich and Howick.[27] By March, however, Buxton, ever driven on by a sense of moral urgency, became impatient with the government's slow deliberations. He let it be known that he would bring forward a motion in parliament on 19 March for the abolition of slavery.[28] Buxton's manœuvre had served its purpose, for Althorp then announced that the government would have on 23 April its definitive word on a plan for abolition. After three months of vacillation, Buxton had secured a pledge that the measure would be speedily introduced.[29]

Pledges made in March that would not be put into effect until April did not make abolitionists terribly optimistic. Once again, as was true during the parliamentary campaign of 1832, the Anti-Slavery forces applied new tactics of popular pressure to insure government action. Throughout the early months of 1833 they had continued to submit petitions to parliament. Anti-Slavery societies were urged to write to

[26] Buxton, *Memoirs*, p. 260; Le Marchant, *Althorp*, pp. 469–71; W. L. Burn, *Emancipation and Apprenticeship in the British West Indies* (London, 1937), p. 105. Government insecurity over the proposed emancipation plan was also recorded by another contemporary chronicler, Thomas Raikes, *A Portion of a Journal Kept by Thomas Raikes, Esq. from 1831 to 1847*, 2nd edn (London, 1856), vol. I, pp. 145, 157.

[27] Jones, *Prosperity Robinson*, pp. 226–7; D. J. Murray, *The West Indies*, p. 193; Thomas Raikes, *A Portion*, vol. I, p. 167. He reported that 'the government asserts that the country demands the abolition of slavery'.

[28] Hansard, *Parliamentary Debates*, 3rd series, vol. 16, pp. 825–6.

[29] Ibid., vol. 16, pp. 1188–9. On 28 March, in the House of Lords, Earl Grey did not commit the Government to that date.

their MPs on the question. Dissenters were particularly active at this time. An editorial in a radical Nonconformist publication, *The Christian Advocate*, was reprinted in toto in *The Tourist*. The piece compared the pressure tactics used by the Agency Committee to that of single drops of water dripping on the head of a victim of torture. They made constant pressure which drove the victim mad. It was, after all, the design of the Agency Committee to 'excite our representatives, to a little Anti-Slavery madness', commented *The Christian Advocate*.[30]

While the Anti-Slavery Movement was marshalling its forces, consolidating its strength, and debating the specifics of emancipation, the government took a step that would have a decided influence on the final outcome of the emancipation issue. During the last week in March, Goderich was relieved of his post as colonial secretary and was replaced by Edward Stanley. Stanley was a tough negotiator and not likely to be influenced by the abolitionist allies in the colonial office—Viscount Howick, James Stephen and Henry Taylor—as the government believed Goderich had been.

Stanley was relieved of his post as Irish Secretary because he was hated by the Irish just as his predecessor in the Colonial Office, Goderich, was relieved of his post because he was hated by the planters. But where Goderich was given a safe post free of controversy—the privy seal—Stanley found himself going from one steaming cauldron of political conflict to another. The emancipation controversy had produced a far more formidable and better organized opposition than he had faced as Irish Secretary.[31] Stanley, having just grappled with one piece of legislation on Ireland that was fraught with controversy, was now acknowledged to have the competence to deal with another of equal excitement and conflict.

The West India body agreed to submit another set of proposals on 23 April. In February they had demanded that compensation be based on the 1823 price of slaves (a high), and they reiterated this request in April. They also demanded that slaves be kept in bondage for forty-one years and that compensation be paid immediately. Faced with the conflicting demands of the abolitionist forces for immediate and

---

[30] *The Tourist* (March 1833), p. 268.

[31] Wilbur D. Jones, *Lord Derby and Victorian Conservatism* (Athens, Georgia, 1956), pp. 228–30; Goderich must have had a difficult time bringing the abolitionists and the planters together. He told Buxton just before he resigned that the government could not carry through an emancipation act. Richard, *Sturge*, p. 101. Goderich had a reputation for being timid. Jones, *Prosperity Robinson*, p. 230. It was only after Earl Grey threatened to resign that Goderich relinquished his post as colonial secretary. Thomas Raikes, *A Portion*, p. 175.

unconditional emancipation, and of the West India interest for pro-
longed servitude and high compensation, Stanley postponed his motion
from 23 April to 14 May.[32]

To let the government know that the organization was united on the
question of immediate emancipation, and favoured monetary relief for
the planters, as well as to assure themselves that the provincial committees were supporters of the general policy of the movement, a
national convention of Anti-Slavery societies was organized to meet on
18 April.

A united front behind the most significant question—immediate
emancipation—emerged from the resolutions of the convention when it
assembled in London.[33] Provincial societies sent 330 delegates in all—
an overwhelming response on the national level to the question. Joseph
John Gurney, drafted an address that was presented to Stanley and
Lord Althorp. It favoured 'some kind of reasonable measures for relief
of the planter' provided justice be given to the slave. 'No scheme,'
stated the memorial, 'which would leave him half a slave and half a
freeman would be beneficial.' Immediate and unconditional emancipation was needed.[34]

All 330 delegates that had been assembled for the convention paraded
en masse to Downing Street to impress upon the ministers that the
Society's programme had a national backing. They were given the
ministers' assurances that the government plan would meet with
their approval. The convention took them at their word, and when
it disbanded on 29 April there was strong feeling in the countryside
that emancipation on the Society's terms would be realized. With the
government's plans still not known, it was easy to believe that the
principles adhered to by the Society might be endorsed in some satisfactory way. Many of the delegates were clergymen of the dissenting
faiths. Their assembled numbers produced a moral impact that was
very great.

In late April and early May, Stanley hammered together the government plan. He came to his assignment after having introduced the Irish
Coercion Bill, a very controversial measure that deprived the Irish
of important civil liberties. Ireland, like Jamaica, had been plagued by

---

[32] Le Marchant's Diary, p. 330 included in A. Aspinall (ed.), *Three Early
Nineteenth Century Diaries* (London, 1952). Murray, *The West Indies*, pp. 200–1;
F. J. Klingberg, *The Anti-Slavery Movement in England* (New Haven, 1926),
p. 284; William L. Mathieson, *British Slavery*, p. 231.
[33] *The Tourist* (22 April 1833), p. 300. Richard, *Sturge*, p. 105.
[34] The text of the petition along with a critique of the government plan was
printed in Cobbett's *Political Register*, vol. 80 (18 May 1833), p. 433.

civil disorder. Stanley successfully dealt with the problem there by fashioning a legal instrument that gave the state increased power. He would follow this precedent when dealing with the West Indies. Stanley's plan for emancipation would secure him a second legislative triumph within six months.

The British public's ever greater determination to have emancipation become a reality undoubtedly goaded Stanley on. When he took office at the end of March there was a decided change in the pattern of public petitioning. In all of February and March of 1833 there had been over 150 petitions for emancipation, with never more than 21 presented in one day. On 29 March there were 50 petitions in one day, and on 3 April there were 55. After 15 April the daily average was between 50 and 100 while 200 were presented on 26 April. In the days immediately before Stanley was scheduled to present his plan for emancipation, there were 300 petitions on 3 May, over 200 on 13 May and over 500 on the day that Stanley presented his proposals 14 May. Obviously, the Anti-Slavery organization on the national level had exerted an overwhelming influence. It was able to direct not only members of the Society, but also public opinion, by using the device of a petition (Doc. 7).

The House of Lords was equally deluged with petitions to the same number. On 14 May there were over 600 petitions presented and this was true on 17 May as well. On 8, 9 and 10 May there were over 200 petitions presented each day. Though there was no scheduled debate on emancipation in the Lords, the abolitionist public, ever aware of the conservative character of the upper chamber, was in effect warning them that they were determined to make emancipation a reality. Events from 14 May to 12 August demonstrated that the Lords would take the public outcry to heart on this issue as with no other since 1830. The Emancipation Act was the only piece of legislation to pass the House of Commons during the first session of the reformed parliament that was virtually left unchanged and unaltered by the House of Lords.[35]

[35] House of Commons, *Journals*, vol. 88, pp. 20 and *passim*. The greatest numbers in any one period compared with similar figures for the 1830–1 session (7½ folio pages of petitions listed in the index). House of Lords, *Journals*, vol. 65. Unlike 1830–1 where Anti-Slavery forces had not petitioned the House of Lords at all, there were an equal number of petitions to the Upper House for that session (7½ folio pages of petitions listed in the index). It was an all-time record for the movement to have an equal show of strength in both Houses. Some of the more unusual petitions included were one from the Mayor, Aldermen and Commons of the City of London, 187,000 signatures from the females of England (mentioned in *Sir Thomas F. Buxton*, p. 269) and ten from Birmingham; one each from the Glasgow Political Union and the Political Union of the Working Classes and Others of Loughborough.

Stanley's plan was ready for presentation to the Commons on the evening of 14–15 May. In his speech (which many considered one of the best orations ever heard in the Commons), Stanley noted that, because of the differing outlooks on the part of the West India body and the abolitionists, the question was fraught with difficulties. It was a matter of 'doing some good, at the least risk of effecting evil'.[36]

The 14 May plan proposed that slaves be freed only after they had paid off through their own labour the planters' estimation of their worth. During this time they would neither be completely free nor enslaved but instead be serving an apprenticeship as freemen. Three-quarters of the apprentices' time would be spent working as a slave; the other quarter he would spend working for wages to be used to purchase his freedom. Apprenticeship would last for twelve years and the government would loan the West India body £15,000,000 as an advance on the apprentices' emancipation payment.[37] Stanley's original plan also provided for freedom for children under six years of age and for infants; the appointment of stipendiary magistrates as impartial supervisors of the scheme, and the creation of schools for religious and moral instruction. By far the most controversial of all the proposals was the apprenticeship compensation scheme. Intense parliamentary debates followed before a compromise of sorts was reached (Doc. 8).

What was indeed so strange about the plan was its failure to accede to the most important and insistent demand of both the West India interest and the abolitionists. For the former compensation without strings, preferably in the form of an outright grant, had been of paramount importance. For this, Stanley had substituted a loan that was to be paid back by a most novel and untested method—the wages of apprentices who spent their time working as if they were still slaves. The cry of the Anti-Slavery forces had been for immediate freedom, the liberty of the slave to be established without condition through British law. The canvassing of candidates for election to parliament in 1832 had been directed towards this specific point. The April conference had confronted Stanley directly with a petition embodying this demand. Yet none of the five resolutions proposed as guidelines for emancipation as presented on 14 May established the fact that the slave was unconditionally free. Number one merely stated that 'immediate and effectual

[36] Hansard, *Parliamentary Debates*, 3rd series, vol. 17, p. 1194.

[37] Ibid., pp. 1230–1. Stanley's proposals are also discussed in Klingberg, *Anti-Slavery Movement*, pp. 287–9. Viscount Howick, the prime minister's son, resigned from the cabinet as a protest against Stanley's plan. His criticisms of the plan as well as his own plan were printed in *Corrected Report of the Speech of Vis. Howick in the House of Commons, May 14, 1833, on Colonial Slavery with Appendix Containing Emancipation Plan* (London, 1833).

measures be taken for the entire abolition of slavery throughout the colonies . . .', and though slave children under six were freed, this was a very small percentage of the entire servile population. Still another aspect of the plan which was totally at variance with past demands was the stipulation that local legislatures provide for the religious and moral education of the slaves. After what had happened in Jamaica, this proposal could only be received with great hostility by the Anti-Slavery forces.

The government's original plan, moving as it was towards some kind of undefined middle ground, could please no one. The heavily conservative leaning of Stanley's political style was very much in evidence. Yet because of the radical goal that it sought to achieve even the Tories thought little of the plan. The Duke of Wellington hoped the issue would die out as he was convinced that the whole scheme was impracticable; while the West Indians, in private conference with Stanley, declared that they would be utterly ruined. To them the compensation proposal was 'one of the grossest acts of spoliation that any government had ever brought forward'.[38]

On 13 May the Anti-Slavery Society issued a memorandum which severely criticized the proposals especially in view of the favourable reception given to their petition of 18 April by Althorp and Stanley. 'It is difficult to conceive on what ground Lord Althorp and Stanley . . . should indulge the hope that its framers could regard such a plan with satisfaction, diametrically opposed as it is in some respects, to their solemn principles.'[39] The working-class newspaper, *Poor Man's Guardian*, in an editorial on 15 June, stated that they were 'no enemies of emancipation' but did not wish to see government 'pretend to emancipate one set of slaves at the expense of the English tax-ridden slaves . . .'.[40]

---

[38] Le Marchant's Diary, p. 330 quoted in Aspinall, *Three Diaries*. Charles Greville, *Journal*, p. 159. 'It is so complex in its machinery, that none think it practicable'. Thomas Raikes, *A Portion*, vol. I, p. 187. For other hostile reactions from planters see *The Speeches of Mr Barrett and of Mr Burge at a General Meeting of Planters, Merchants and Others Interested in the West India Colonies, May 18, 1833* (London, 1833), p. 3.

[39] *Anti-Slavery Reporter*, vol. 6, 29 May 1833), pp. 145–8.

[40] *Poor Man's Guardian* (15 June 1833), p. 1. This paper and the *Political Register* were both radical and working class in orientation. While they were avidly for emancipation, they were against compensation. Cobbett wrote an editorial against it on 3 August 1833. At the time that the resolutions regarding emancipation were agreed to, an amendment was proposed in parliament that would stop the government from levying a new tax to pay for compensation. The amendment explained that it was the propertied classes that would benefit from compensation, so it was they that should have its burden. House of Commons, *Journals*, vol. 88, p. 482.

To the more conservative members of the Commons and certainly of the Lords a far greater issue was at stake for them than repressive taxation and the wages of the people, namely, the government's intention arbitrarily to deprive men of their property in whatever form it took. Buxton's moderate amendment to hold back half of the funds until the end of apprenticeship were lost by a large majority (277–142) on 11–12 June. This was an indication that there was a strong political consensus in favour of compensation even among the supporters of immediate emancipation.[41] There were shared values of British society, and the sanctity of private property was one. In June, then, one of the most important ideological stumbling blocks to emancipation had been settled. Private property and the right of British citizens to maintain it was a principle of the British common law. The government had from the beginning of the slave trade until 1833 supported and upheld the right of her citizens to have property in human form—slaves. If a parliamentary act was to deprive certain citizens of their property, government must be prepared to compensate them for the loss. The act of parliament was arbitrarily setting new definitions for private property. Those who were forced to lose this property as a result of the change had a right to demand compensation. Most of the members of the Anti-Slavery Society were in accord with this idea. Their nation had supported the right of citizens to hold property in men. This was a national sin and had to be accepted and dealt with because it had always existed. The institution of slavery was perpetuated by the entire nation and supported by its laws, and the country should make some financial sacrifice to see this shared national crime abolished.[42]

Buxton, defeated on compensation, fought on for securing a still more important victory for Anti-Slavery forces—unconditional and immediate emancipation. The major contingency blocking this was the apprenticeship. The problem had been fully discussed in a series of meetings called by the Anti-Slavery Society on 14 May to discuss the minister's plan.

Related to the issue of Negro labour were the specific terms of the apprenticeship. Convinced by the West Indian interest that the Negro would remain idle unless the compulsion of servile labour was maintained for a period of time, Stanley had designed its terms so that the Negro would be working as a slave, without wages. Abolitionists argued that, as apprentices, they were neither free nor slave, and, having wages that were small and inconsequential, they would feel no compulsion to work.

[41] *Journals*, ibid., p. 476. A grant of £20,000,000 was approved.
[42] Resolutions of the Anti-Slavery Society at meetings held on 14 May, 1833, reprinted in *Anti-Slavery Reporter*, vol. 6, p. 152.

Give them their liberty and pay them wages, they argued, and the problem of work habits and discipline would vanish. Drop the notion of apprenticeship, and a 'potent remedy' for all the vices of slavery could be found in transforming the former slave into a free labourer. The results would be 'a kind of social and economical regeneration' which would create a positive outlook towards work.[43] At the end of June Stanley agreed to the proposal that immediate emancipation be conceded to the slaves before their apprenticeship.

In the interim between the discussions of May and June on the principles of the bill and the start of the debates on specific clauses, Stanley asked James Stephen to draft the legislation. For Stephen this was a memorable task. He was the son of one of the original founders of the movement, James Stephen, and the brother of George Stephen. As the only abolitionist in the Colonial Office, he was greatly honoured to draft the instrument of Negro emancipation. With an energy which reflected his dedication to the cause, Stephen drafted the entire statute of sixty-four clauses in one week-end.

The bill was read for the first time in parliament on 5 July.[44] Buxton's strategy throughout was the try to change the specific clauses of the bill that were repugnant to the Anti-Slavery viewpoint. Buxton, Lushington, and others in parliament saw no reason to reject the entire measure. Believing that the Negro's welfare was the greatest factor involved and that he would have everything to gain should he be given his freedom whatever the contingencies, Buxton decided to fight the apprenticeship clause after the bill had passed its second reading. Before its final approval it would face the scrutiny of the House of Commons in Committee of the Whole. Then he felt the Anti-Slavery forces should 'muster all our strength for the most vigorous opposition to the objectionable clauses, and if we direct it judiciously and exert it fully', they would bring positive results.[45]

In all probability, Buxton was further hampered in his efforts to modify the emancipation bill by the counter efforts of the Tories to have the measure thrown out in its entirety. The titular head of the Tory party, the Duke of Wellington, had been a strong opponent of the abolitionists throughout his parliamentary career. He had long resented the political power that the Anti-Slavery movement wielded in parliament. Along with Lords St Vincent, Penshurst, and Wynford, the Duke was to

[43] *Anti-Slavery Reporter*, vol. 6, p. 149. Davis, *J.N.H.*, vol. 46, pp. 173, 169.
[44] Ibid., vol. 6 (6 July 1833), p. 165. Mathieson, *British Slavery*, p. 240.
[45] *Sir Thomas F. Buxton*, p. 277. George Stephen, *Anti-Slavery Recollections*, p. 202. Klingberg, *Anti-Slavery Movement*, pp. 296–9.

enter a petition of dissent against the Emancipation Act after it had already been approved by the House of Lords (Doc. 9).

Both Buxton and Thomas B. Macaulay expressed deep concern over the future of the emancipation bill in letters written during the week of 12 July. Buxton declared that 'the fact is that critical as has been the state of our great cause before, perhaps never was it so critical as now'. The measure, had reached the 'crisis of its fate'. Macaulay fully expected the government to resign that week because of the intense hostility of the House of Lords to its legislative programme. The obstructionist tactics of the Lords would prevent the slavery bill from passing.[46] Because of these obstacles the second reading of the Emancipation Act was postponed, not once, but four times.

On 23 July, the day of the second reading, a major defection in the abolitionist ranks was brought before parliament. Adam Hodgson, chairman of the Committee of the Liverpool Anti-Slavery Society, entered a petition against the slave abolition bill requesting that it would not pass as it stood. For a rare moment in the political life of the Anti-Slavery movement, the great unity of the membership with its leaders had been shattered.[47]

Buxton, having dealt with these pressures for many months, knew that the emancipation issue had reached a critical juncture. Just before the debate on apprenticeship, he and thirty-three MPs requested a private meeting with Stanley. Two hours of argument could not change the government's position. Stanley was adamant in his refusal to alter the provisions of the apprenticeship. The warning of Buxton and other MPs that the 'country will be dissatisfied, and we must appeal to it' could not force his hand. As far as Stanley was concerned, the future of the government bill for the abolition of slavery rested with the apprenticeship issue. 'The apprenticeship must stand, or the bill must go with it,' he told them.[48]

Despite Stanley's adamant stand, Buxton still believed that there was sufficient strength in parliament to change the apprenticeship clause. And his perception of the mood of parliament on this issue was acute. He all but secured the passing of a clause that would have abolished apprenticeship. On 24 July 1833 his motion that an apprenticeship be

---

[46] T. F. Buxton to W. L. Garrison, 12 July 1833, reprinted in *The Liberator*, vol. 3 (9 November 1833). *Sir Thomas F. Buxton*, p. 282. Thomas B. Macaulay to Zachary Macaulay (13 July 1833) in Viscountess Kutsford, *Life and Letters of Zachary Macaulay* (London, 1900), p. 471. For Wellington's petition, see House of Lords, *Journals*, vol. 65, p. 604.

[47] House of Commons, *Journals*, vol. 88, p. 592. On 1 August a petition from Dublin called for immediate and unrestricted emancipation.

[48] George Stephen, *Anti-Slavery Recollections*, pp. 204–5.

limited to 'the shortest period which may be necessary to establish on just principles, the system of free labour for adequate wages' was defeated by seven votes.[49] The Anti-Slavery forces had succeeded in bringing in a tally that could have defeated the government.

Of all the measures proposed by Buxton to modify the Emancipation Act, the one on apprenticeship of 24 July brought the greatest show of parliamentary strength for the abolitionist forces. It was hardly expected by the government that this clause would be supported by a majority of seven. Stanley, according to parliamentary tradition, was in fact defeated by this vote, but he chose not to resign. Instead, heeding the mood of parliament somewhat, he consented to have the apprenticeship reduced from twelve to seven years so that it would end in 1840. Because of the unexpected show of strength, Stanley was forced to modify his position.[50]

An analysis of the vote of 24 July reveals where the greatest strength of the movement lay. There was formidable Anti-Slavery strength in the new boroughs. Fifteen out of the twenty-two largest boroughs had one or two MPs who voted with the abolitionists. Birmingham, Leeds, and Manchester had both their MPs voting against the government, and these cities were the largest in the nation outside the capital. By contrast, not one of the MPs from the city of London was swayed to the abolitionist camp, but its suburb, Greenwich, had two MPs who were staunch abolitionist supporters. Some other, newly created parliamentary boroughs that sent at least one MP to parliament who voted against the government were Devonport, Sheffield, Bath, Brighton, Blackburn, Lambeth, Stoke-on-Trent, Ashton and Bolton.

All of the new boroughs, whatever their size, were strongly committed to the Whig party. They also had large numbers of £10 freeholders. Middle class in their orientation, they were the chief beneficiaries of parliamentary reform. The 50 per cent increase in the electorate in the boroughs that resulted from the Reform Bill was solidly in the abolitionist camp. Out of forty-one new boroughs that were created by the Reform Act, twenty-seven had MPs committed to oppose the government on the apprenticeship issue.

[49] Hansard, *Parliamentary Debates*, 3rd series, vol. 18, p. 1192. *Sir Thomas F. Buxton*, pp. 277–9. On the Saturday preceding the crucial vote, there was a mass meeting at Exeter Hall. Over three thousand people attended, many from out of town. During the meeting, sixty-six MPs gave their pledges to support the Anti-Slavery position on the apprenticeship issue. This was but a foreshadowing of the greater strength that the abolitionists would demonstrate in the parliamentary test. Stephen, *Anti-Slavery Recollections*, p. 205.

[50] Hansard, *Parliamentary Debates*, 3rd series, vol. 19, pp. 1218, 1220–338. Stephen, *Anti-Slavery Recollections*, p. 206.

The thirty-eight boroughs with one or two MPs in support of the abolitionists which were the same as they had been before 1832 were representative of a variety of differing communities. There were tiny boroughs that had escaped reform like Cockermouth, Buckingham and Totnes; they had between two hundred and three hundred electors. In all three both MPs voted against the government. Two small cities, Pontefract and Poole, had MPs who voted with the abolitionist forces. There was strong support in the sea coast towns of the nominally conservative south: Bath, Truro, Plymouth, Barnstaple, St Ives. Leicester had a large number of dissenting congregations. Both its MPs supported the abolitionist position. The majority of the boroughs of this category had populations ranging from four thousand to fifteen thousand.

In the counties there was considerable strength in Yorkshire where three out of five MPs supported the cause. In Buckinghamshire, Kent, Somerset, Leicester and Surrey there were at least two MPs who supported the motion. These counties had large numbers of dissenting congregations. There were twenty-six MPs from the counties who supported the abolitionist position.

It is interesting to note that the techniques of organization and propaganda were effective at every population level and in every type of community in England. In the newly enfranchised and represented towns like Birmingham and Manchester, where the level of political organization was very high, the abolitionist movement was equally effective. But even in the smaller towns, and in some of the tiny boroughs where the tradition of political protest manifest in the larger towns hardly existed, abolitionist strength was decisive.[51]

As the bill stood after the crucial vote of 24 July, the planters were securing compensation. Yet as the radical abolitionists saw it, the slave was not getting his freedom. The Anti-Slavery Movement had been persuaded to accept compensation as the price of freedom. But if compensation did not in fact purchase freedom, there was little point in giving in to the planter's demand. Hence the stand that Buxton took on 31 July when the specific clause relating to compensation was debated.

On the morning of this debate, Buxton was urged by George Stephen,

---

[51] This analysis is based on the following sources: the list of votes for and against as printed in Hansard, *Parliamentary Debates*, 3rd series, vol. 18, p. 1219. *The Extraordinary Black Book*, John Wade (ed.) (n.d. ed., 1832, reprint 1970), pp. 85, 611–15. This last listed the counties and boroughs, old and new, their populations and how they were represented in the pre-reformed and in the reformed parliament. There was also a list of counties and the number of dissenting congregating in each one.

James Cropper, Joseph Sturge and others to 'fight the money battle and defeat Mr Stanley if possible'. He made no pledge to do so. During the discussion, however, it was clear that Buxton did his best to change the terms of compensation. He tried to tie it to a change in the apprenticeship.[52] His motion of 31 July proposed that, rather than pay the funds in toto to the planters, half of it was to be paid when the Emancipation Act went into effect and half at the end of the apprenticeship.[53]

Stanley was aghast at this latest ploy of the abolitionist forces. He had always won his points without threats. Even the events of 24 July, though somewhat startling to the government, had left him in complete control. He had made some compromise, however slight, on the terms of the apprenticeship. When Buxton and Lushington sought to revive the whole issue once again using the compensation terms as a means for their ends, Stanley was enraged. Compensation had been a basic tenet of any settlement of the issue. The House had already agreed in the resolutions of 12 June to £20,000,000 in compensation. Stanley could only feel that it was bad faith for the Anti-Slavery leaders to try, at the last minute, to change the terms of the settlement. He warned the House that the entire bill would be endangered if Buxton's motion was agreed to. He threatened to resign and withdraw the government's support. Buxton, Stanley exclaimed, would be left to carry it through on his own. The House, he believed, was bound in honour to give full and complete compensation at once. Stanley's threat could not hold back the opposition to compensation. Buxton secured 93 votes for his motion as against the government's 144.[54]

Buxton had carefully maintained the confidence of the government throughout the political struggle. He had acted as a moderating influence among the more radical ranks of the organization. It is of great significance that the parliamentary leaders and their entire Anti-Slavery following in the Commons openly opposed the government and actually risked the defeat of the entire emancipation bill. Zealous leaders and their

[52] *Sir Thomas F. Buxton*, p. 279. Davis, *J.N.H.*, vol. 46, p. 169 states that this meeting was on 24 July, but as the compensation issue was debated on 31 July, the meeting most probably took place on the morning of 31 July.

[53] Hansard, *Parliamentary Debates*, 3rd series, vol. 20, p. 208. The same manœuvre had been tried on 12 June and had failed. House of Commons, *Journals*, vol. 88, p. 476.

[54] Hansard, *Parliamentary Debates*, 3rd series, vol. 20, p. 219. Before the debate Buxton was well aware that Stanley would resign if defeated. *Sir Thomas F. Buxton*, p. 279. It was only after he had been defeated on the compensation issue that Buxton voted with the government for the entire amount. He did not fear Stanley's threats or a slave uprising, as assumed by Burn, *Emancipation*, p. 117.

followers might have destroyed the emancipation of the slaves had the Anti-Slavery forces triumphed in that division of 24 July and certainly in the one of 31 July. The political skill with which Buxton and Lushington had overseen the entire parliamentary fight would have been for naught. They too were driven to change their tactics because of the overwhelming zeal of their followers.[55]

'I thought it right . . . to persevere', Buxton wrote to a friend on 1 August, 'but I must confess that I should have felt anxious if we had obtained a victory.' At the risk of defeating the entire measure which surely was a cause for anxiety, Buxton stood for principle alone. The controversial debate, he reported to his friend, 'was one of the best we have ever had'.[56] On 7 August, one minor change was extracted from Stanley. A clause which guaranteed that no slave would be made to work on Sunday, so that he would be free for religious worship, was approved. Efforts by the only Methodist in the House, Mr Wilks, to get stronger penalties for the destruction of missionary chapels and to have funds put aside for the education of the slaves were put down. The government, Stanley announced, would work out in the Commons a separate plan on education, for this was not directly connected with the terms of emancipation.

The bill then went to the House of Lords where it was opposed in no uncertain terms by the titular head of the Tory party, the Duke of Wellington. He described the haste in which the bill was being considered and presented petitions against it from Jamaica. Wellington's hatred of the Dissenters was apparent when he tried unsuccessfully to strike out a clause which extended the protection of 52 George III to the colonies. He obviously was no friend of religious liberty either at home or in the colonies. For this law guaranteed the right of religious worship to Englishmen regardless of denomination. Apart from Wellington's vocal and very determined opposition, which was supported by the

[55] Stanley's success, reported *The Eclectic Review*, was due to the lack of informed opinion on slavery in the House of Commons. 'The movements of parties under such circumstances', concluded the *Review*, 'must be regulated very much by the fugleman', vol. 10 (10 October, 1833) p. 320. A modification in the apprenticeship plan through amendments which would require the planters to pay them wages or prohibit the punishment of the whip for idleness or neglect of work was lost by comfortable margins. House of Commons *Journals*, vol. 88, p. 611.

[56] *Sir Thomas F. Buxton*, p. 280. Referring to Wellington's opposition, Thomas Clarkson later wrote to Buxton that 'I tremble to think what might have been the consequences if you had refused the proposals of the government'! ibid., p. 283. On 2 August, the decision was to pay the compensation from the General Fund of Great Britain and Ireland. House of Commons, *Journals*, vol. 88, p. 629.

bishops of the Anglican Church, the bill passed the Lords without any major changes.[57]

After the reform bill controversy, George Stephen believed that the peers could recognize a popular issue when they saw one. Thus the Tories refrained

> from trial of strength; the Peers had not yet forgotten their self-exile from their own House on the reform bill, and they were not yet inclined to a second struggle with the people.[58]

Though the law was not to become effective until 1 August 1834, with the King's assent given on 26 August, the emancipation of the 800,000 slaves had become a legal reality (Doc. 10).

At the very time that parliament succeeded in having slavery abolished in the West Indies, conservatives had been able to keep East Indian slavery from meeting the same fate. Here is but another striking proof of the relationship between the methods employed by the movement to bring about their goals and the corresponding successes that they achieved. The East Indian Charter Bill was committed to the abolition of slavery in India. When the charter renewal for the East India Company was introduced into parliament at the same time as the abolitionist bill, the slavery provisions were diluted. This purpose was easily subverted by conservatives in both houses. The government plan had called for the abolition of slavery in East India Company territories without compensation by 12 April 1837. But this radical provision was quickly transformed as the bill made its way through parliament. First the terminal date was removed, and then wide discretionary powers were given to the Indian authorities as to how the provision should be implemented. Like West Indian policy in 1823, emancipation was to be gradual in India. Programmes for ameliorating the slaves' conditions were to be introduced. Preoccupied as the abolitionist forces were with securing a just measure for emancipation in the West Indies, they did not employ the same pressure tactics used for the Emancipation Act to the East Indian Charter Bill.[59]

[57] Hansard, *Parliamentary Debates*, 3rd series, vol. 20, pp. 338, 409. There was also no official effort in parliament to change the provision of the bill which allowed each colonial legislature to draft its own emancipation act though the animosity of the movement towards them was very great. However, on 24 July both Buxton and Lushington criticized this provision in the House of Commons: vol. 18, pp. 1060 and 1185.

[58] *Anti-Slavery Recollections*, p. 207.

[59] Howard R. Temperley, *British Anti-Slavery 1833–1870* (London, 1972), ch. 5. In 1840–3 the movement's campaign to abolish slavery in East India and Ceylon brought about its legal abolition in those territories. The act of 1833,

With Britain and her citizens rested the enormous guilt of having initiated and maintained a slave trade and then of having created and maintained a slave society in the West Indies. To have wilfully inflicted this status on fellow beings was a great wrong that Britain and her citizens were liable and accountable for. To have deliberately sinned and flagrantly abused God out of selfish motives for mere self-gain was the most intolerable crime of all.

Thus the movement mounted a campaign to abolish slavery. Because the Anti-Slavery ideology had presented slavery as a crime that had been committed and perpetrated by the British people and its government, they were more deeply concerned for the moment with emancipation in the British West Indies. By contrast, slavery in India was of the Indians' own creation. Great Britain had found it there. Thus the abolition of slavery in the East was not a first priority for the movement.

The issues in the debate which climaxed with the successful passage of the Emancipation Act did not die miraculously with the new law. Though Bermuda and Antigua answered every abolitionist's prayers by immediately doing away with apprenticeship through local statute, there were still Jamaica, the largest by far of the slave societies, and the lesser islands to contend with. The failures of the apprenticeship scheme would become more apparent after 1834 when the Emancipation Act went into effect. Once again the movement, as had been true in 1831–3, was driven by a great sense of moral urgency to do away with the system. Once again the support of the public would be successfully enlisted. Only the group of leaders was somewhat changed. The organization that they all had been a part of was to be reformed into new groupings.[60]

In July 1833, Wilberforce died. But the other senior leader of the movement, Thomas Clarkson, would live on until 1846. In April 1833, Clarkson had answered the optimistic and idealistic pronouncements of a woman abolitionist who hoped he would live to witness

---

however, provided emancipation for the slaves of Mauritius and the Cape of Good Hope. British North America was not even mentioned in the act, though it applied there as well: Robin Winks, *The Blacks in Canada: a History* (New Haven and London, 1971), p. 111.

[60] At first, the Anti-Slavery Society did advise the slaves to 'patiently wait for the hour of full emancipation'. While apprentices they should 'maintain an undeviating submission to the laws'. In parliament Buxton had declared, 'trust implicitly to that great nation and to that paternal government who are labouring for your release'. *Anti-Slavery Reporter*, vol. 6, pp. 221–32. George Stephen carefully pointed out that the workers in the movement after 1833 were with one or two exceptions (Joseph Sturge, George Stacey) not the same as those of the old Anti-Slavery committees. *Anti-Slavery Recollections*, pp. 210–11.

universal emancipation with 'I have no expectation of it'. In September 1833 all this had changed. He wrote to his old friend William Smith, who had been a parliamentary spokesman for the movement since 1787, that 'we may leave the world with an assurance, that slavery has now received what will be its death blow in every part of the world'.[61]

Committed to an evangelical vision of world-wide Christianity, pledged from the start to the belief in a universal God whose egalitarian nature made him available and accessible to all men, Anti-Slavery forces sought to find still more converts for that God. First in their own empire among the slaves in the West Indies, Mauritius and the Cape of Good Hope. Then they set about almost immediately to find other areas to get the same results through the same means. The United States with its large slave population was an obvious target. At the same time that they sought universal emancipation, the Anti-Slavery forces could not delude themselves about the conditions in the British colonies. They had foreseen these realities and must again work to change them. The problems connected with the British emancipation act were not yet over. The failure of apprenticeship was already apparent. Negroes, aware of their status as freemen, no longer wanted to work as slaves. Planters were treating them cruelly. There was a continued decline in authority relationships. The pledge of the 339 delegates in April 1833 to effect immediate emancipation was yet to be redeemed. Freedom for the slaves was in name only.

Buxton did not participate in the parliamentary battle that was to be taken up against apprenticeship. In the general election of July 1837, he was not re-elected. The mantle of leadership fell to Joseph Sturge and his associates in Birmingham. They sent out a call for a national conference of Anti-Slavery leaders which was convened in London on 14 November. Out of the conference emerged a new organization—the Central Emancipation Committee—whose objective was to force the government to terminate apprenticeship immediately. Joseph Sturge emerged as the leader of the fight. The new committee adopted the techniques of mass agitation of the old Agency Committee.

The new parliament was hardly receptive to the Anti-Slavery cause. Buxton had lost his seat, and he believed that there were not a hundred men in either House who would support a plan for the abolition of apprenticeship. Nevertheless, Sturge, who had always found Buxton too

---

[61] Thomas Clarkson to 'Madam' (15 April 1833), John Rylands Library, Manchester. Thomas Clarkson to William Smith (1 September 1833), Perkins Library, Duke University. Clarkson also wrote to Buxton that he was pleased with the Emancipation Act although 'it was not entirely' what he had wished, *Sir Thomas F. Buxton*, p. 283 (see Doc. 11).

cautious, compromising and conservative in his outlook, was determined to take action. The Central Committee resolved to secure the total and unconditional abolition of the apprenticeship system by August 1838.

The events of 1837–8 were almost a rerun of 1832–3. Once again agents were sent throughout the countryside to contact the Anti-Slavery public. Meetings were held and the older leaders as well as many new ones took the cause to heart once again. Indignation was high as there was widespread belief that the planters had cheated the people. £20,000,000 had been spent to redeem the slave's freedom and in fact he had not secured his freedom at all. The absolute power of the owner over the body and soul of another man had not been broken.

Once again there were corresponding moves in parliament followed by a mass meeting in London. On 20 February 1838, Brougham proposed in the Lords that apprenticeship be terminated on 1 August 1838. He found almost no supporters. With no hope in the Lords, the Central Committee turned to the House of Commons. A mass convention of 364 delegates organized by the Central Emancipation Committee met in Exeter Hall on 27 March 1838.[62]

While the convention was still in session Sir George Strickland, MP from the Anti-Slavery stronghold of Yorkshire's West Riding, moved in parliament on 29 March that apprenticeship should cease on 1 August 1838. Public opinion was reflected in the vote on what must have seemed to the government a rash proposal. With the leaders of both parties against it, the motion secured 215 votes out of a house of 484. The lobbying, petitioning and public clamour that were as intense as 1833 produced comparable results. Sturge and his associates considered this vote to be a moral triumph. England, the *Spectator* reported, was 'in convulsions' over the apprenticeship issue.

Encouraged by their strong support in the Commons in March, Anti-Slavery leadership in parliament decided to try again. Sir Eardley Wilmot notified the government that he would make a motion in parliament on 22 May for the immediate abolition of apprenticeship. Once again the usual pressure tactics were brought to bear on the MPs, and for the third time in six months a mass convention was assembled in London to support the motion.[63]

[62] Richard, *Sturge*, pp. 166–8. For Buxton's cautious approach, see his correspondence with Sturge as reported in Temperly, *British Anti-Slavery*, pp. 32–5 and *Sir Thomas F. Buxton*, pp. 359–60.

[63] Richard, *Sturge*, pp. 169–71. *Sir Thomas F. Buxton*, p. 361. Temperley, *British Anti-Slavery*, p. 38. Burn, *Emancipation*, p. 352. As in the days of 1833, there was mass petitioning in 1838. On one day in March, 250 petitions were presented in the Commons.

On 22 May, as a result of a snap decision in a thinly attended House of Commons, a resolution by Sir Eardley Wilmot in favour of ending apprenticeship on 1 August was actually approved by a small majority. However, the action was later stayed as a result of government intervention.

In order to effect a compromise with the powerful Anti-Slavery following in parliament, the government put a law through parliament in April 1838 which modified the apprenticeship provisions of the Emancipation Act. It gave the colonial governors greater powers to deal directly with the abuses of the apprenticeship. It also deprived the planters of the right to use the whip as punishment and prohibited all punishments of females. Fear of encroachment on their political power forced the Jamaica legislature to take another look at the apprenticeship issue. Rather than have their political power weakened by a strengthened, powerful governor, the legislature decided to do away with apprenticeship through a local statute. Other islands—Nevis, Virgin Islands, Granada, St Vincent, St Kitts, Barbados, British Guiana, Tobago, the Bahamas, Dominica—were equally wary both of having a strong governor and of the failure of the system.

The agitation of the Central Emancipation Committee had succeeded. Without direct parliamentary intervention, the islands had abolished their own apprenticeship two years before the termination date set by statute. Once again the Anti-Slavery forces had been successful in creating a public victory on a moral issue. And once again, cheered on by their great victory, they returned as they had in 1833 to future goals.[64] (An Order in Council issued in August 1838 abolished apprenticeship in the crown colonies.) And thus inserted in the history book of the British Empire, one chapter—bondage—was forever closed and a new one—freedom—was just beginning.

[64] Mathieson, *British Slavery*, pp. 296–311. Burn, *Emancipation*, pp. 354–6. Hinton, *Knibb*, pp. 243–51.

4

The Anti-Slavery Movement and British Society

In the slave society power relationships between the lowest rank on the social scale and the highest were completely unbalanced. The rulers of that society had unrestrained and unmitigated control. There was little sense of responsibility on the part of the slave-owner or his hired supervisor with regard to the use of power. The slave was subject to every kind of degradation, punishment and the ever present possibility of death. Neither his owners nor their hired hands needed account for their actions. They had no inner restraints of conscience. And the local community, government and society at large offered no effective censorship to the use of this power. West Indian slave society was lacking in a responsible elite. Power had no social controls. Estate managers, the hired hands of the absentees, were totally without restraint in the way in which they used it. Racism provided further justification for this attitude.

Yet another difference between the landowners of the West Indies and those in England was that the majority of landowners of the West Indies were not residents of their islands at all. To them their plantations were merely economic enterprises. Being absentee owners in Jamaica, St Kitts or Barbados carried no particular civic obligation to those island societies. Thus, though the West Indian islands were peopled and exploited by England, the notion of property there evoked different expectations and demands.

The nature of property was radically different too. The property that meant wealth in the slave society was land and human beings. The possession of a sugar estate in the West Indies had little value unless it was worked by slaves. Human property involved possession of the life and soul of the individual. There were few opportunities for patriarchal or paternalistic behaviour when the majority of persons living in the island society were property to be exploited. And people could be exploited mercilessly because they were viewed as beasts of burden rather than human beings.[1]

In England, after the Glorious Revolution, a patriarchal and paternalistic aristocracy prided itself on its responsible use of power. Until the end of the eighteenth century, British society looked to its aristocracy with the expectation that it would use its power, whether it be in the community or in the political institutions, responsibly. With three quarters of the members of parliament landowners, the aristocrats possessed total political control. Yet power was mitigated by the paternalistic traditions of British society. In the hierarchical order each group had its place, its prescribed functions and its responsibilities, and society. Here was a huge concentration of power in the hands of the few—the very few. Yet, unlike the slave society's elite, they did not abuse their power to irretrievable lengths. Or if they did, there were built-in controls of government and society which were theoretically available to restrain them. It was the failure of these controls to affect the behaviour of Englishmen in the colonies that brought about the formation of the Anti-Slavery Movement.

While both the slave society and British society were hierarchical, as power was equated with landed wealth, each society's expectations of their hierarchies were quite different. In England, power carried with it a sense of community obligation. The largest landowners had the greatest responsibility; they wielded the political power and were rulers of society. And down the ladder, the smaller landowner, the merchant, the manufacturer, the peasant, all who possessed property linked their status with a responsible role in society. There were also methods of sharing power between groups. Patronage was the way in which the political aristocracy spread its favours to greater numbers. And in the local communities in particular gentlemen of wealth and standing often helped and aided the less fortunate. Political favours came through local friendship. There was a large degree of integration among community members.[2]

During the early decades of the nineteenth century, English society in general was rapidly changing and individuals' values were being tested as never before. Moral discipline, discipline based on the inner controls of conscience, emulation and self respect, was subject to stress.

[1] For the abolitionist critique of the slave society: William Wilberforce, *An Appeal To The Religion, Justice, and Humanity of The Inhabitants of The British Empire, On Behalf of the Negro Slaves* (London, 1823). Zachary Macaulay, *Negro Slavery* (London, 1823), James Stephen, *British West Indian Slavery Delineated*, 2 vols (London, 1824–30) (see Doc. 2).

[2] Harold Perkin, *The Origins of Modern English Society* (London, 1969), pp. 17–56.

God was, in the final analysis, the strongest paternalistic power of all. As the Nonconformist middle class more and more lost faith in the paternalism of the aristocracy, it found still greater confirmation in the belief that God was the highest authority. To the Quakers, the 'inner light' shone for all. Just as the slave society denied the vast majority of its members the inner moral discipline that comes after a commitment to faith which creates a relationship with God, so English society was in constant need of this moral discipline. It could only be acquired through a reaffirmation of faith.

Both the slave society and English society were in need of greater authoritative regulation from within. Mutual recognition of this need would enable them both to cope with changes in the social order.

In the view of the abolitionists the failures of the slave society were most apparent and manifested themselves most gravely in the lack of religious community. Its rulers did not wish to have Christianity brought to their slaves. Rather they often actively prevented missionaries from bringing the word of God to the Negroes. Lack of concern for Christianity was reflected in the behaviour of the slave-owners. They had no restraints of conscience or inner moral controls. Slaves were mercilessly exploited, women were used as concubines, and family life was destroyed. The slave society had a tyrannical, amoral leadership that subverted and corrupted Christian values. Their crimes were further compounded by their great hostility against those seeking to bring Christianity to the islands—the missionaries. The men who ruled the slave society proved also to be a conspiratorial oligarchy which deliberately used despotic means to deprive the slaves of a religious life, a moral life. They made a mockery of Christian values. Their attitudes towards those who were the agents of God, the missionaries, showed that they themselves were incapable of grasping the ethics of religious culture.

As the abolitionists saw it, a society which produced a ruling class displaying in its behaviour towards the Negro no moral values of its own was a society that did not deserve the protection and support of the British government. In their literature on slavery, the slave trade, and slave society, the movement sought to show what happens to men who have no moral values. Using as evidence the accounts of those who had lived and worked in the West Indies, they proceeded to demonstrate what the corrupt values were and how they affected the behaviour of those in the slave society.

As was true of the literature of the evangelical revival in general, there was nothing terribly exciting or radically different in their views of Christianity. To those who believed, truth was self-evident. The purpose of both the revival literature and the Anti-Slavery propaganda was to reaffirm man's faith. What Wilberforce said in his *Practical View* about the evangelical frame of mind was apparent in the literature. He believed that 'It must be the business of their whole lives to grow in grace, and continually adding one virtue to another . . .'[3] To crusade against slavery was a virtuous act which would bring praise from the Almighty; it was a practical way to re-affirm the self-evident truths of revealed religion. The literature provided a guide for supporting the intense earnestness and narrow focus of the cause.

The Anti-Slavery Movement appealed to the religious denominations that were already rooted in moral communities to reach out to the slaves, to help them find religion. Their goal was to create a Christian moral community in the slave society. By appealing to the Christians of all persuasions, the movement enlarged and made more powerful the moral thrust of English society. It provided a means for bringing together many Christian communities into a united and all powerful whole. Every person who was committed to the Anti-Slavery crusade transcended himself not only as an individual but as a member of a religious faith to unite with all faiths against a common enemy.

English society had many religious institutions that were significant components of its culture. There was an established Church which fused the political apparatus with the theological apparatus at the pinnacle of state power. This meant that theoretically the ideals of Christianity were supported and defended by the state. Great Britain was a Christian nation, not only because the majority of its citizens were of the Christian faith, but also because the Anglican Church shared directly in state power and wealth.

On an equally significant level of religious expression were the flourishing Protestant sects that had originated during the course of the seventeenth century. Baptists, Quakers, Presbyterians, Unitarians and Independents had important followings among the middle class. In 1739 Methodism was born, brought about by the preaching of the great evangelist John Wesley. Here, as with other sects, the teachings of Christ were poured into still another type of vessel for dissemination among those who were yet uncommitted. Christianity was thus, both in its sectarian and in its established form, a component institution of English culture.

The Anglican evangelical revival with its condemnation of the slave

---

[3] William Wilberforce, *A Practical View of the Prevailing Religious System of Professed Christians in the Higher and Middle Classes in this Country, Contrasted with Real Christianity* (London, 1797), pp. 50–1.

society by leading evangelists, such as Wilberforce, provided the political leadership for the development of an Anti-Slavery organization on a national level. They were backed by Quakers, Methodists and Baptists. Wesley had condemned slavery as had Abraham Booth, the foremost Baptist ideologist. Political pressure was exerted by evangelists, though much of the organizational strength and financial support was supplied by the Nonconformists. Members of dissenting sects— Quakers, Presbyterians, Methodists, Baptists—were deprived of political and religious rights, excluded from the universities and from military service. Their identity as members of society was derived from their religious affiliation. They were profound believers and were devoted to the evangelical notion of the egalitarian relationship between God and man. The dynamic nature of their religion was a fitting complement to the innovative spirit of their work.[4]

In contrast to the latitudinarian attitude of the Anglican Church, Dissenters throughout the eighteenth century had cultivated a narrow spirituality which reflected an attitude of obedience to God and His moral order without question. Many Dissenters were from yeoman stock, the lower levels of the propertied middle rank who, in contrast to the freewheeling, indulgent aristocracy, were traditionally men of the most pious nature. By the end of the eighteenth century a new generation of Dissenters was born who did not feel the psychological stigma that Nonconformity had held for their parents. Their worldly success made them ever more committed to the belief that their religious outlook was a superior one. With the expansion of their economic power came an ever greater commitment to support the expansion of their church. They were independent of the Establishment and wanted to remain that way.

In terms of physical growth, non-Anglican places of worship expanded enormously during the first half of the nineteenth century. There were 7,116 non-Anglican places of worship licensed between 1688 and 1770, while between 1771 and 1830 there were over 32,000 such places of worship or meeting places so licensed. Methodists of all connections experienced the greatest growth, Baptists and Independents were next. In contrast there was no corresponding growth in the Anglican Church. The complacency of the Church hierarchy, comfortably shielded from criticism by the state, offered little to the dynamic new class.

[4] John H. Overton, *The Evangelical Revival In The Eighteenth Century* (London, 1907), p. 133 and *passim*. John Wesley, *Thoughts on Slavery* (London, 1774). Abraham Booth, *An Essay On The Kingdom of Christ* (London, 1788). W. T. Whitley, *A History of British Baptists* (London, 1923), p. 277.

Dissenters had been instrumental in fostering much of the innovative spirit that had taken hold of English society from the eighteenth century onward. Methodists emerging from the evangelical revival, inspired by Wesley and Whitefield, attracted large numbers of Anglicans. Baptists also experienced a revival at the end of the century. In 1813 they formed a General Baptist Association and were like the others active in the moral reform societies of other Nonconformists and of the evangelical Anglicans. In the course of the eighteenth century, Dissenters had been transformed from subordinate peoples to assertive and dynamic minorities. They were uncompromising in their search for excellence in all aspects of life, and religion was of the utmost importance.[5]

Their religious organizations were always non-violent and their concept of social change was couched in religious terms. Their devotion to the slavery issue was derived from their great individual emphasis on conscience. They were energetic in the pursuit of its moral dictates. Quakers, Methodists, Baptists, and Independents were zealous in their pursuit of religious self-expression. This showed itself in several ways. Their own churches received their spiritual and financial support. The denominations were the backbone of the missionary societies, Bible societies and societies for the repression of vice, and the like. The Anti-Slavery Movement had supplied them with one of their first political causes.[6]

The Quaker commitment to both the abolition of the slave trade and the abolition of slavery brought the sect into contact with the evangelical outlook of other Dissenters and the Anglicans. Hitherto Quakers had never been a sect that proselytized. They had confined the impact of religious doctrine to their own closed circle. Evangelical doctrine, which they came to understand and adopt through their support of the abolition issue, won many converts among them. The result was a broadening of outlook. As they fought for the freedom of the slave so that he could come to God, they found they could support evangelical ideology as it applied to other religious reforms at home. Friends became supporters of the missionary aspects of Christian life because of the slavery controversy. By the 1840s evangelical theology had come to influence the outlook of English Friends and thus they remained most loyal to the Anti-Slavery ideology.

The attitude of the Quakers changed from aloofness to deep commitment to politics. Their wealth and religion freed them to work for

[5] Harold Perkin, *Origins*, pp. 191–209. 'Religious Worship in England and Wales', House of Commons, *Accounts and Papers*, vol. 39, 1852–3, *passim*.
[6] Ford K. Brown, *Fathers of the Victorians* (Cambridge, 1961) and David E. Swift, *Joseph John Gurney: Banker, Reformer, Quaker* (Middletown, 1962).

international causes. The weekly meeting and the national conferences were the only formal obligatory religious functions. Their strong stress on individual excellence and religious perfection produced both a single-minded piety and a great moral drive. There were no ministers or other professional leaders of the group. As each man and woman was to be his or her own minister, each was free to minister to others. With a minimum of formal service required in their own organizations, Friends could devote themselves to other far-reaching religious causes. Hence their devotion to the Anti-Slavery work.[7]

There were many areas of British life which Dissenters sought more and more to criticize and reform. They sought political and religious equality. While demanding complete religious freedom for themselves, they demanded the same for the slave.

Dissenters' identity with the slave was so complete that the numbers of petitions presented to parliament in favour of emancipation were far greater than the petitions presented for repeal of their own civil disabilities. In 1827 petitions presented in the House of Commons for the repeal of the Test and Corporation Acts numbered two and a half folio pages. The petitions presented for the emancipation of the slaves in the Commons in 1830–1 numbered seven and a half folio pages and the same again in 1833. In 1833 an equal number of petitions were presented in the House of Lords for the emancipation of the slaves. Part of the success for the numbers of petitions presented must be attributed to the great organizational work of the Agency Committee. But inasmuch as the majority of its committee members and stipendiary agents were ministers or members of dissenting faiths, the identity and impact of the leaders and their followers were one.[8]

All economic, social and religious strata supported emancipation. None petitioned as members of the Anti-Slavery Society although many undoubtedly were. They preferred instead to stand with their own particular religious affiliation, town or sex. Most identified their commitment to emancipation with their religious affiliation although economic status was sometimes a factor. Their sense of self-definition was thus completely linked to their indictment of slavery. Their own traditions were linked and continued to be linked to the oppressed. The Dissenters' cry of protest was not only for slaves but themselves.

An analysis of the vote in parliament of 24 July when Buxton sought

[7] Edward Grubb, *Quaker Thought and History* (New York, 1925), pp. 76–7. Swift, *Gurney, passim.* John S. Rowntree, *Quakerism Past and Present* (London, 1859), p. 133–6.
[8] House of Commons, *Journals*, vol. 82 (1826–7), index; vol. 88, index.

to do away with the apprenticeship clause further reveals the great Dissenter commitment to the movement. In the most conservative unit of representation—the county—there were over twenty-five MPs who voted with Buxton against apprenticeship. With the exception of two counties, all of the others contained over one hundred dissenting congregations. Yorkshire in the West Riding had, since 1830, been an important centre of abolitionists feeling, and had 1,019 dissenting congregations. It had the largest number of Quaker congregations of any county and the largest number of Methodists and Baptists. As a result, not only did the two MPs from the West Riding, Morpeth and Strickland, vote with the abolitionists, but one MP from East Yorkshire, Alderman Thompson, supported them as well. Of the other counties that had two representatives and had voted with the Anti-Slavery party, Somerset had 254 dissenting congregations, Kent 210, and Buckinghamshire 121. There the Tory Marquis of Chandos was obliged to vote with the abolitionists though he had opposed the Reform Bill in 1832.

One county to elect an MP of dissenting faith—Durham—had 177 dissenting congregations, mainly Methodist, though their MP Joseph Pease was a Quaker. Thomas Gisborne, who was active in the Anti-Slavery Society from 1823, was elected from the county of Derbyshire North that had 182 dissenting congregations—the third largest group in the kingdom. Three counties that returned one MP and were solidly Anti-Slavery, yet had dissenting congregations of one hundred or less, were Huntingdonshire with thirty-six, Berkshire with eighty-one, and Cambridgeshire with eighty-five.

Many of England's largest towns which had important dissenting populations allied with the Anti-Slavery Society, and voting with them on the apprenticeship issue were Manchester, Leeds, Birmingham, Stoke on Trent, Leicester, Sheffield, Liverpool, Brighton, and Bolton. These people exercised the franchise as residents of independent boroughs for the first time in 1833, and the backbone of their electorate was Nonconformist. Thus by the time the decisive issue—emancipation—had been put to the test of the electorate, the movement had called up powerful support among the Dissenters. It had always had the backing of the Quaker elite and to a lesser degree of one or two Baptists or Methodists, but by 1832 their mass support could not be doubted.[9]

[9] This analysis is based on the following sources: the list of votes for and against as recorded in Hansard, *Parliamentary Debates*, 3rd series, vol. 18, p. 1219 and *The Extraordinary Black Book*, John Wade (ed.), (London, 1832, reprint 1970), pp. 85, 611–15.

As in the cities, in the countryside Methodists, Baptists and Independents dominated the religious scene. These Dissenter congregations had still more meeting places in the countryside than in the towns. Both the North Riding and the West Riding of Yorkshire had large numbers of Wesleyan Methodist meeting places greater than those of York itself. The religious pattern of worship dominant in the largest towns was decidedly dissenting, and most particularly Methodist, Baptist and Quaker. Methodists had been committed to an Anti-Slavery stand from the inception of the movement. Baptists and Independents were next in importance in the religious population of the towns and they were decidedly Anti-Slavery. Methodist strength was greatest in the towns which had between 20,000 and 100,000 persons. They were second only to the Church of England (by a small margin) in towns of 100,000 or more. It was these towns that benefited from the Reform Bill and whose MPs supported the apprenticeship stand of 24 July 1933.[10] The appeal of the movement to constituencies throughout the kingdom was on religious grounds. The Agency Committee took pains to inform its lecturers and representatives that their appeal should be solely on moral terms. Nonconformists, who were the backbone of the movement's support in the small cities and in the industrial towns, became passionate believers in emancipation. Knibb and the other stipendiary agents made it clear that the 1831 rebellion and the response of the rulers of Jamaica had confirmed beyond doubt the abolitionists' most fundamental criticism of the slave society. The oppressor's lack of moral restraint and his omnipotent power were a source of destruction of Christian principles and disruption of the moral order. The oppressed were helpless before this power. As a safeguard against this violence, Zachary Macaulay had in 1832 proposed that any plan for emancipation provide for a paid judiciary and strong police force. Its personnel would include free Negroes, whites and 'the most intelligent and religious of the present slaves'. A racially mixed force would be effective not only to keep order but 'still more the whites, in complete submission'.[11]

In December 1832 the Committee of Deputies of Protestant Dissenters in a memorial addressed to the government concerning the rebellion noted that it was a threat to the rights of the Nonconformist public. Throughout the 1820s missionaries had been attacked by the planters. Dissenters and their allies feared greater catastrophic events

---

[10] House of Commons, *A and P*, vol. 39, 1852–3.
[11] Samuel and Isaac Wilberforce (eds.), *Letters of William Wilberforce* (London, 1840), vol. II, p. 525.

which would endanger or totally wipe out the religious rights of their constituents. They did not fear violence from the slaves but from their masters. The security of every Dissenter was threatened by the events in Jamaica.[12] The Jamaica Rebellion of 1831 and the reaction of the planters raised the spectre of religious persecution as never before. These persecutions had once been the lot of Nonconformists in England. It had once been their historical fate. The disabilities they were subject to were symbolic of the greater intolerance with which they had been treated in the past. The fate of the slave was once their fate. They must seek greater religious freedom for themselves and at the same time bring the black man to the point where he could enjoy the privileges that were already theirs.

Political and religious institutions had interfered with their own religious rights. They were attracted to the abolitionist movement because its ideology made them aware not only that the slave society failed to provide access for man to come to God, but also had prevented the slave from receiving his forgiveness. The slave too had been deprived of religious self-expression.

Nonconformists faced vast inequities in their pursuit of religious expression. They supported the Anglican Church financially when paying tithes in their localities. They were required to marry in Anglican chapels only and to be buried in Anglican churchyards. Nonconformists were also barred from admission to Oxford and Cambridge universities. They were discriminated against and kept down by a repressive social order.[13]

Their positions paralleled that of the slave. Just as the Anti-Slavery forces had been attacking the slave society for its failure to promote Christian marriages, so one of the major grievances of the United Committee of Dissenters in 1833 was that the compulsory Anglican marriage ceremony be done away with. Just as they had criticized the administration of the West Indian islands for its failure to keep an accurate registration of births and deaths while denying its Negroes the right to Christian burial, so the Dissenters' grievances of 1833 had listed absence of legal registration for births and deaths and denial of burial rights in parochial churchyards as grievances that must be redressed.

---

[12] Thus it was not 'Emancipation from below' that was their fear, as assumed by Eric Williams, in *Capitalism and Slavery* (Chapel Hill, 1944, reprint 1961), p. 208.

[13] Norman Gash, *Reaction and Reconstruction in English Politics 1832–52* (Oxford, 1965), p. 66. Elie Halévy, *The Triumph of Reform* (London, 1950), *passim*.

The abolitionist ideology had been severely critical of the British state. It had attacked its support of the slave society on moral grounds. The hostility which the Nonconformists felt for the state could find a direct outlet in the Anti-Slavery movement. If the British state was sinful because of its protection and encouragement of the slave society, was it not equally to be damned for discrimination against non-Anglican Christians?

The Tories, the party of the high church, were protective of the power that the Nonconformists wished to destroy. Because of the heavily liberal-Whig parliaments in 1833, they made their influence felt more effectively in the House of Lords where the former prime minister, the Duke of Wellington, was their political spokesman. As the bishops also had seats in the Lords and were staunch conservatives, the Tories did all they could to block church reform. It was in the Lords that the Reform Bill and the Emancipation Act had been strongly opposed. The Anglican establishment and their Tory protectors were in favour of continued state discrimination against Dissenters. They had a vested interest in maintaining them as well as the Jews as second class citizens. The opposition to emancipation had been put down; the opposition to religious reform would not be overcome for most of the nineteenth century.

The political battles of the Dissenters and the enslaved black man began at the same juncture in history. Wellington attributed the electoral defeat of his Tory party in 1833 to its failure to attract the votes of the Dissenters. He expected that they would continue to oppose the Tories, it was reported by Lord Ellenborough, 'until they have accomplished their ends, which are the destruction of the church and Negro emancipation'. This arch-conservative was well aware of the intimate connection between the Dissenters' zeal both for the reform of the Church (which would give them greater freedom of religious expression) and the Emancipation Act.[14]

Dissenters were confronted with the spectre of the Anglican Church whose oligarchic powers were supported by conservatives in both

---

[14] A. Aspinall, *Three Early Nineteenth Century Diaries* (London, 1952), p. 310. Wellington's biographers have either failed to mention or not analysed his strong opposition to emancipation. The latest in a long list is Elizabeth Longford, *Wellington, Pillar of State* (London, 1972). In more than 400 pages devoted to Wellington's political exploits there is not even a sentence on it.

In a tract defending the prejudices of Jamaican slave society, a leading planter Richard Barrett exclaimed 'You hate a Jew much, a Unitarian a little more than a Jew, and a Roman Catholic you both hate and fear.' *A Reply to the Speech of Dr Lushington in the House of Commons on June 12, 1827 on the . . . Free Coloured People of Jamaica* (London, 1828).

parties. The Church's power was all but omnipotent; the state re-enforced its impregnable position. Nonconformists, then, could well understand the kind of oppression faced by the slave. They too were deprived of religious self-expression by the state. The Anti-Slavery Movement sought to free the slave from the omnipotent oppression of the master. With the abolition of slavery missionaries were free of persecution. They could work freely to help the slave find a religious identity of his own. After the Reform Bill of 1832 Nonconformists sought to enhance their own religious status in the state. They engaged for the first time in a political struggle with the state for freer expression of their religious identity. As abolitionists they had worked for the right of the Negro to have a religious life of his own. As citizens of Great Britain they sought greater status and greater religious self-expression for themselves.

English society, like the slave society, was insensitive to the religious needs of its people. Negro slavery conformed to the inherited image of the anti-Christ; it awakened the millenarian fantasies of persecution and suffering. Nonconformists could identify with the slaves on these grounds. Slaves were powerless in the face of this threat as Nonconformists were. The Anti-Slavery Movement was a vehicle for bringing to the surface internal strains and conflicts of British society.[15] The Dissenter-Establishment battle was one of the greatest political conflicts of the nineteenth century.

Like Dissenters, women could find in the slave society the perfect image of tyranny and despotism greater, powerful and more enormous for them perhaps than the tyranny of the established Church. Family life was destroyed, women had no influence over the rearing of their offspring. Females were exploited both economically and sexually by the authority figures of the slave societies. They were also subject to cruel physical punishments deliberately inflicted. The Anti-Slavery Movement made much of this issue. The exploitation of women was a grave offence, at the heart of the moralistic indictment of the slave society. The pages of the *Anti-Slavery Reporters* were filled with authentic descriptions of feminine travails and exploitation. The slave society denied women all aspects of maternal leadership, direction and discipline. The ladies of Britain could abhor this and want to see it changed. All those who were enslaved suffered, but women suffered

[15] For a general discussion of the impact of reform movements on liberal society cf. David Brion Davis, *The Slave Power Conspiracy and the Paranoid Style* (Louisiana, 1969), pp. 76–86. For a discussion of the religious conflicts of the nineteenth century cf. G. Kitson Clark, *The Expanding Society* (New York, 1967), and Gash, *Reaction and Reconstruction*.

still more. No middle class women would want to have their maternal role denied them if they came from the religious-minded public—the backbone of the Anti-Slavery Movement. The intertwining of their religious selves with their identity as women was so complete that their commitment was as members of religious denominations and as women. In their petitions to parliament, women would often identify themselves as the women of a given town. Their male counterparts would have a separate petition, though both groups were members of the same church. In the Christian universe women's role was carefully defined. Their responsibilities were significant; theirs was a status of great importance. Women crusaded against slavery with these ideological beliefs.

Women's natural dispositions were, according to popular belief, well-suited for the tasks connected with the Anti-Slavery crusade. The 'allowed' or acceptable emotions associated with women's character in those times included an ability to pity the suffering and relieve the miserable. Women were considered to be more sympathetic and kind. As the agents of education for their children, they were closer to the innocent and hence the purest conception of God.

Feminine devotion, loyalty and responsibility for carrying through these tasks was an important example to men. They had no part to play in the false glories of war, destruction and the intense conflicts which pitted men against their fellow men. Free of these entanglements that threatened the moral order, they could pursue a life dedicated to the finer things that led to peace and godliness. Women earnestly sought this pattern of behaviour in their lives. Men could only benefit from this example.

Women's intense involvement in the Anti-Slavery crusade was rooted in the attack on their self image which came from the power structure of the slave society. When, on 10 May 1833, the 'Ladies of Lyme Regis' petitioned the House of Lords for the abolition of slavery, they stated that the system:

> practically insults the feelings of every female on earth and necessarily tends to prevent the cultivation of those feelings of delicacy in the Negro female character in the West Indies without which women, instead of rising to the condition which God designed her to occupy would remain in a state bordering on that of brutes that perish.[16]

Anti-Slavery tracts written in the 1820s often addressed themselves

---

[16] House of Lords, *Journals*, vol. 65 (10 May 1833), p. 284.

directly to women for theirs was a special interest in getting slavery abolished. It destroyed the virtue of the young, as its work of moral deterioration was never-ending. 'An Appeal to the Hearts and Consciences of British Women' was issued from Leicester in 1828. 'If women of cultivated minds, of leisure and influence, decline to exert their talents in awakening the attention and influencing the practice of their less enlightened countrywomen—if women professing godliness stand aloof .. will it not be sin ?' Another tract assured women that 'feminine modesty' would not be offended if they advocated the cause to friends and family or met with ladies in the neighbourhood to make plans. 'Can a woman be reproved for stepping out of her character and becoming a political character if the cause of innocent persons be involved ?' The tract was designed to 'answer objections of women who don't want to join the anti-slavery society'.

Ladies were advised to form associations among themselves, to teach their children to hate slavery and to bring petitions to the legislature and to use only sugar grown by freemen. Theirs was a special responsibility of rescuing not only themselves but their children also from the curse and guilt of slavery. During the height of the emancipation controversy in 1833, George Thompson addressed 1,800 ladies of Glasgow. He was enthusiastic about the outpouring of feminine support. 'The women of England and Scotland are coming forth in the might of their majesty and mercy, and the fervour of their zeal must soon dissolve the fetters of the slave.'[17]

Women's organizations reached national proportions. This was reflected in the petition of the females of Great Britain that was presented to both houses of parliament in 1833. It had over 350,000 signatures on it and was assembled by two Quaker women. Indicative of the large numbers of women that must have been in attendance at previous meetings was that the *Anti-Slavery Reporter* pointed out that at the 2 August meeting of the Society held in London of the 3,000 present there was an 'unusually large proportion of men'.

This comment was in keeping with George Stephen's admission that 'none of our anti-slavery meetings were well attended until after it was agreed to admit ladies to be present'. It was the women who brought the men out to attend. They were successful in convincing their husbands and brothers of the importance of the issue. They were also committed from the late 1820s to the most radical of solutions, as the list of con-

[17] George Thompson, *Substance of an Address To The Ladies of Glasgow and Vicinity on Negro Emancipation* (Glasgow, 1833), p. 6. *Dialogue Between a Well Wisher and a Friend to The Slaves In The British Colonies*, by 'A Lady' (n.d.).

tributors to the Agency Committee coffers was dominated by various ladies' Anti-Slavery societies.[18]

Quaker women were often instrumental in organizing ladies in their localities whether they were members of the Society of Friends or other interested parties. Women had always had equal responsibilities in the organizational framework of the Society of Friends. Since Friends from the earliest beginnings had been strong supporters of the Anti-Slavery Movement, women would naturally play an important role. Methodists, like Quakers, had also looked at women in a more egalitarian light, and this was true of the other dissenting sects that had played an instrumental role in the Anti-Slavery crusade. The movement gave women the opportunity to enlarge their regularly defined sphere of activity and influence. If all were equal before God, then all could equally do God's task. Anti-Slavery was God's work and women took up its challenge with great enthusiasm. They mingled with those of like mind and there, among other women, developed a sense of collective conscience. Women could do with great competence what had hitherto been defined as a man's job. The masculine leadership of the movement began after 1828 (when the first women's societies were formed) to depend on them ever more. As reformers, women had taken on men's work and had proved highly competent in performing these tasks.

It was the male-led Agency Committee and its stipendiary speakers that provided the public image of the professional agitator. However, much of the back-up work in terms of fund raising, distribution of literature, and securing petitions was done by women. They were the ones who, through their own segregated societies, brought the Anti-Slavery message most effectively to their local communities. Women thought it in the realm of their accepted mode of behaviour and way of life to take whatever measures they could to destroy slavery.

As homemakers women had the responsibility of seeing that the family did not consume slave-grown sugar. Literature of all kinds was made available through an Anti-Slavery lending library. Not only did they distribute the tracts, but they also provided the funds to have additional copies printed and distributed in their neighbourhood. They met in each others' homes and read the *Anti-Slavery Reporters* and other tracts aloud. They sought to influence their children to hate slavery and to teach them to love the great family of mankind. These

[18] George Stephen, *Anti-Slavery Recollections* (London, 1854), pp. 197-8. *Report of the Agency Committee of The Anti-Slavery Society Established June, 1831* (London, 1832), Appendix.

were all activities that could be performed within the domestic setting that was the middle class woman's environment.

Content with the fundamental role that they held within the Christian universe, British women abolitionists allowed their male counterparts their superior status within the organization. Thus it was American women who having recently dealt with male prejudices against feminine equality in abolitionist societies, who likewise challenged the male chauvinist practices of the English movement at the World's Anti-Slavery Convention in 1840. (Women could not participate with men.) These women, among them Lucretia Mott and Elizabeth Cady Stanton, were also to be founders of the women's rights movement in America. It was their experience at the Convention which added the fuel to the fire which just eight years later, in 1848 blazed forth as the Women's Rights Convention in Seneca Falls, New York.[19]

Though Elizabeth Pease Nichol and Ann Knight, two of the most devoted feminine abolitionists at the World's Convention, were sympathetic to the demands of their American counterparts and were made aware as never before of the oppression of women, there was no radical change on their part to new reform programmes. It was not until 1866 (after the Civil War) that the majority of British feminine abolitionists turned their attention to reform activities for women's rights. Except for Miss Knight who in 1851 organized the Sheffield Political Union, her comrades preferred to devote their women's organizations to the abolition of slavery in America.

Slavery within the British Empire had been abolished, yet British women continued to put the oppression of others under slavery, no matter how far or removed, before their own. Between 1833 and 1865 feminine abolitionist societies were organized in major cities such as London, Birmingham, Bristol, Leeds, Edinburgh and Glasgow. They lent moral support in numerous letters which crossed the Atlantic. Much needed cash contributions and other material support were also given. Deep friendships particularly with William Lloyd Garrison and his followers were cherished and nurtured by both parties. Because of the high status given to women as the guardians of the moral order and the conservative evangelical tradition of the British movement's Quakers and other Nonconformists, the movement's feminine wing remained exclusively devoted to that calling.[20]

[19] Frederick Tolles, *Slavery and the Woman Question: Lucretia Mott's Diary* (Pennsylvania and London, 1952). Elizabeth Cady Stanton *et al.*, *History of Woman Suffrage* (New York, 1881–7), vol. I. pp. 70–1.

[20] Caroline A. Biggs, 'Great Britain' in Elizabeth Cady Stanton *et al.*, *History of Woman Suffrage*, vol. III, pp. 838–42. Helen Blackburn, *Women's Suffrage*

In general Nonconformists took all the important leadership roles in the British Anti-Slavery Movement by 1840. The Anglican evangelical political elite that had been in the forefront of the movement since 1787 prevailed as public leaders through the resolution of the emancipation issue.

Nonconformists came to the fore as the leaders of the British and Foreign Anti-Slavery Society. Founded in 1839, it was headed by Joseph Sturge, the radical Quaker who had been the leader in the apprenticeship fight of 1838. Even before the BFASS the new organization which immediately replaced the old Anti-Slavery Society, the Central Emancipation Committee, and the British and Foreign Society for Universal Emancipation, were of a different composition from that of the earlier national Anti-Slavery organizations. Whereas the Society for the Abolition of the Slave Trade and the Anti-Slavery Society formed in 1823 for the gradual abolition of slavery had had their share of both honorary and active supporters among the benevolent Anglican aristocrats, the new organization was exclusively Nonconformist and most particularly Quaker in character. The emancipation issue had brought this middle class group of Dissenters to the fore. They had played a significant role in politics for the first time after 1833 and continued to dominate the movement. Not that they weren't a significant element before. In 1787 all but three of the original members of the Committee for the Suppression of the Slave Trade were Quakers. What was unique about the post-emancipation period was that Quakers and other Nonconformists no longer left the public leadership to the Anglicans and other members of the Establishment. They were ready to supply not only the monetary support and manpower for the movement, but become the movements' exclusive leaders as well.[21]

From its origins the Anti-Slavery Movement was dominated by evangelical Anglicans and Quakers. These had the most conspicuous leadership roles in the Anti-Slavery Movement. Quakers enjoyed a greater degree of religious freedom and independence and wealth than other Nonconformist sects. Theirs was a self-image of a pious Christian elite. Secure in their belief that the 'inner light' of God dwells in every man, they had the confidence to bring it to all.

The BFASS was in effect an instrument of individual evangelical

(London, 1902), p. 55, 96–100. *William Lloyd Garrison, 1805–1879: The Story of His Life As Told by His Children* (New York, 1885–9), *passim*.

[21] Christine Bolt, *The Anti-Slavery Movement and Reconstruction* (Oxford and New York, 1969) and Howard R. Temperley, *British Anti-Slavery 1833–1870* (London, 1972), *passim*.

expression towards the oppressed and enslaved black man. Most of its monetary support was derived from the large contributions of benevolent Quakers. Its second greatest source of support was from small individual contributions, while in its auxiliary societies over a half to two thirds of the Society's income came from the Society of Friends.

The particular expression of philanthropic piety that was characteristic of the BFASS was not confined to that group alone. There were provincial Anti-Slavery societies in Glasgow, Edinburgh, Dublin and Manchester which developed their own Anti-Slavery programmes and policies.

The Anti-Slavery Movement, as it emerged from the emancipation decade of the 1830s, would, as a result of the change in the composition of its national leaders, be effective in a different way than it had been in earlier decades. In the past, because of the political prominence of its earlier leaders, it had had a significant impact on parliament and the English government. After 1840 the political effectiveness of the movement was seriously curtailed. Dr Stephen Lushington was the only member of the parliament on the board of the BFASS, but he rarely attended meetings, and, when he retired from parliament in 1841, there was no other politician to replace him. While William Evans and Lord Brougham were often available to speak for the Anti-Slavery cause in parliament, they did not take an active role in the policy formation of the BFASS. Sir Thomas Fowell Buxton, who remained in parliament until 1845, took no political role either in the organization's formation or in its policy programmes.[22] He concentrated his efforts in parliament on the abolition of the international slave trade. Thus he returned to the original objectives of Wilberforce and the other founders of the movement. Like them he espoused the development of Africa as a solution to the problem.

The BFASS with its Quaker dominated, evangelically inclined leadership focused its efforts on the abolition of slavery throughout the world. It sponsored the World's Anti-Slavery Convention of 1840. Opponents of servitude from the United States, France and Great Britain dominated the London meeting. They met to delineate the problems facing the opponents of slavery throughout the world; and they were formidable! In the western hemisphere there were 2,750,000 slaves in the United States, 2,500,000 in Brazil, 600,000 in the French Colonies, 100,000 in the Dutch and Swedish Colonies and 25,000 in Texas. In

[22] In a letter to Henry Crabb Robinson he explained that he would probably not attend the World Anti-Slavery Convention of 1840 as its objects were 'quite distinct from mine' (10 June, 1840). University College, London.

the eastern hemisphere there was slavery in India, and those enslaved in the colonial possessions of France, Holland and Portugal.

After 1840 the BFASS and the independent organizations had a wide range of issues to deal with. There was the movement's long-standing problems related to the international abolition of the slave trade and the state of Negro life in the liberated colonies. The question of worldwide emancipation was a fundamental concern. The new leaders were guided much more by the instincts of the evangelists rather than the expertise of the politician. Their single-mindedness which boarded on fanaticism did not weather well in the fray of the political arena. Their efforts in furthering the international and colonial development of the Negro did not have the impact on society that the movement to abolish slavery within the British Empire had had.

The political failures of the Dissenters in their battle with the Anglican Establishment left them still an oppressed minority. Their strong support of the Anti-Slavery Movement's worldwide crusade was but a continued expression of their identity with other souls who were kept from free religious expression and oppressed by oligarchies. Joseph Sturge, who learned the ropes of political agitation in the Anti-Slavery crusade, tried his hand at a political career. He allied himself with the Chartists and sought election to parliament twice in the 1840s. He failed to win either election. Sturge preferred to give his attention to the slavery question and his BFASS rather than to the political issues at home.[23] Dissenters were not yet ready to play a leading political role in the affairs of state. They felt most comfortable in asserting their Christian identity in religious causes. 'Their education,' noted the *Eclectic Review*, 'does not fit or dispose their more opulent or leading men to devote themselves to the thorny and precarious pursuit of politics. Their resources, their energies, their enterprise, their public spirit have been expended on other objects ... those of enlarged philanthropy or religious benevolence'.[24] The slavery question was one they remained particularly close to throughout the nineteenth century.

The Reform Bill of 1832 made it possible for Nonconformists in the newly created parliamentary boroughs and in the smaller towns and counties to raise their political voice in 1832–3. Their assertion of their religious demands and identity before a hostile political order was a manifestation of the self-confidence that their class had developed in

---

[23] Temperley, *British Anti-Slavery 1833–1870*, chs 3 and 4. G. D. H. Cole, *Chartist Portraits* (London, 1941) presents a particularly succinct summary of Sturge's political career.

[24] This is the interpretation of Norman Gash, *Reunion and Reaction*.

British society. The bigoted and conservative Tory High Church Alliance had opposed the abolition of slavery, for they refused to acknowledge the demands of those who sought religious equality in their own society or in the slave society. Yet ruling elites were forced to respond. The Emancipation Act was their first affirmative support for that principle. The shared ideological values of the evangelical Anglicans such as Zachary Macaulay, William Wilberforce, the Stephens and Thomas Fowell Buxton created an integrating mechanism which allowed them to work together with the Dissenters. Their political status and skills made it possible initially to facilitate the integration of the demands of Dissenters with the hostile political order.

Dissenters were in complete control of the Anti-Slavery Movement after their Anglican evangelical counterparts had rested their case against slavery on the grounds of moral nationalism rather than moral internationalism. They used the Anti-Slavery Movement to proselytize for their God, to fight for the right of his spirit to live in the hearts of all men. Even after emancipation had been achieved in Great Britain, the dictates of their religious creed made it imperative that they bring the spirit of their saviour of those still enslaved and those once enslaved throughout the world.

The outpouring of public protest against slavery in 1830–3 was greater than any protest against religious discrimination in the whole of the nineteenth century. Dissenter sense of security and self was not derived from an external identification with the alien Anglican order but from an internal single-minded identity with God. They behaved according to the discipline of their faith. Committed to an evangelical interpretation of Christianity, theirs was an egalitarian vision of a universal God.

Both evangelical Anglican and Dissenter claimed that the ideological shared values of British society legitimized a vision of moral equality. The British power structure, based as it was on the unity of protestantism with the political state should, they believed, support that ideal. When it was apparent at the time of the slave trade controversy and again at the emancipation crises that the reactionary forces were rooted in those elements that were at the pinnacle of the Church-State hierarchy, evangelicals of the Anglican persuasion threw in their lot with the Dissenters. Within the liberal political environment they fought together and triumphed.

Great Britain, the world's first industrial society, was also the first industrial nation voluntarily to abolish slavery. The underlying cultural ethos of the protestant state rested on the assumption that there was a universal God available to all. The Anti-Slavery Movement revitalized this ideal and gave it a dynamic thrust forward. Despite the uneven distribution of economic and political power within the British state, the social transformation that had taken place as a result of the industrial revolution forced its elites to be more tolerant of the part of their Christian tradition that was not in accord with their own self image.[25] Even the all powerful elites of the slave society were forced, as a result of the emancipation act, to respect that tradition. Within their particular social worlds these elites could never really accept that tradition; yet they very reluctantly acquiesced in the legitimate claim it had on the political state. When slavery was abolished in the empire, Britain became the first nation state to translate into legislation the notion of equality of all the world's races and peoples.

[25] It was a synthesis of social and ideological values that caused the downfall of slavery in Great Britain. Whether it was profitable or unprofitable to British capitalism, as strongly suggested by Eric Williams, *Capitalism and Slavery*, was not the point at issue. Nor did the movement cease to lose interest in the slaves after 1833. See pp. 126, and especially 135–6 and 191.

DOCUMENTS

I. FROM William Wilberforce, *An Appeal To The Religion, Justice and Humanity of The Inhabitants of The British Empire On Behalf of the Negro Slaves in The West Indies* (London, 1823)

But though the evils which have been already enumerated are of no small amount, in estimating the physical sufferings of human beings, especially of the lower rank, yet, to a Christian eye, they shrink almost into insignificance when compared with the moral evils that remain behind—with that, above all, which runs through the whole of the various cruel circumstances of the Negro slave's condition, and is at once the effect of his wrongs and sufferings, their bitter aggravation, and the pretext for their continuance,—his extreme degradation in the intellectual and moral scale of being, and in the estimation of his white oppressors.

The proofs of the extreme degradation of the slaves, in the latter sense, are innumerable; and, indeed, it must be confessed, that in the minds of Europeans in general, more especially in vulgar minds, whether vulgar from the want of education, or morally vulgar, (a more inwrought and less curable vulgarity,) the personal peculiarities of the Negro race could scarcely fail, by diminishing sympathy, to produce impressions, not merely of contempt, but even of disgust and aversion. But how strongly are these impressions sure to be confirmed and augmented, when to all the effects of bodily distinctions are superadded all those arising from the want of civilization and knowledge, and still more, all the hateful vices that slavery never fails to engender or to aggravate. Such, in truth, must naturally be the effect of these powerful causes, that even the most ingeniously constructed system which humanity and policy combined could have devised, would in vain have endeavoured to counteract them: how much more powerfully then must they operate, especially in low and uneducated minds, when the whole system abounds with institutions and practices which tend to confirm and strengthen their efficiency, and to give to a contemptuous aversion for the Negro race, the sanction of manners and of law. . . .

The first particular of subsisting legal oppression that I shall notice, and which is at once a decisive proof of the degradation of the Negro race, in the eyes of the whites, and powerful cause of its continuance, is of a deeply rooted character, and often productive of the most cruel effects. In the contemplation of law they are not persons, but mere chattels; and as such are liable to be seized and sold by creditors and by executors, in payment of their owner's debts; and this separately from the estates on which they are settled. By the operation of this system, the most meritorious slave who may have accumulated a little peculium, and may be living with his family in some tolerable comfort, who by long and faithful services may have endeared himself to his proprietor or manager,—who, in short, is in circumstances that mitigate greatly the evils of his condition—is liable at once to be torn for ever from his home, his family, and his friends, and to be sent to serve a new master, perhaps in another island, for the rest of his life.

Another particular of their degradation by law, which, in its effects, most perniciously affects their whole civil condition, and of which their inadequate legal protection is a sure and necessary consequence, is their evidence being inadmissible against any free person. The effect of this cannot be stated more clearly or compendiously than in the memorable evidence of a gentleman eminently distinguished for the candour with which he gave to the Slave Trade Committee the result of his long personal experience in the West Indies,—the late Mr. Otley, Chief-justice of St. Vincent's,—himself a planter:—"As the evidence of slaves is never admitted against white men, the difficulty of legally establishing the facts is so great, that white men are in a manner put beyond the reach of the law." It is due also to the late Sir William Young, long one of the most active opponents of the abolition, to state, that he likewise, when Governor of Tobago, acknowledged, as a radical defect in the administration of justice, that the law of evidence "covered the most guilty European with impunity."

The same concession was made by both houses of the legislature of Grenada, in the earliest inquiries of the Privy Council. The only difficulty, as they stated, that had been found in putting an effectual stop to gross and wanton cruelty towards slaves, was that of bringing home the proof of the fact against the delinquent by satisfactory evidence; those who were capable of the guilt, being in general artful enough to prevent any but slaves being witnesses of the fact. "As the matter stands," they add, "though we hope the instances in this island are at this day not frequent, yet it must be admitted with regret, that the persons prosecuted, and who certainly were guilty, have escaped for want of legal proof."

It is obvious that the same cause must produce the same effect in all our other slave colonies, although there has not been found the same candour in confessing it.

The next evil which I shall specify, for which the extreme degradation of these poor beings, in the eyes of their masters, can alone account, is the driving system. Not being supposed capable of being governed like other human beings, by the hope of reward, or the fear of punishment, they are subjected to the immediate impulse or present terror of the whip, and are driven at their work like brute animals. Lower than this it is scarcely possible for man to be depressed by man. If such treatment does not find him vile and despised, it must infallibly make him so. Let it not however be supposed, that the only evil of this truly odious system is its outraging the moral character of the human species, or its farther degrading the slaves in the eyes of all who are in authority over them, and thereby extinguishing that sympathy which would be their best protection. The whip is itself a dreadful instrument of punishment; and the mode of inflicting that punishment shockingly indecent and degrading. The drivers themselves, commonly, or rather always slaves, are usually the strongest and stoutest of the Negroes; and though they are forbidden to give more than a few lashes at a time, as the immediate chastisement of faults committed at their work, yet the power over the slaves which they thus possess unavoidably invests them with a truly formidable tyranny, the consequences of which, to the unfortunate subjects of it, are often in the highest degree oppressive and pernicious. No one who reflects on the subject can be at a loss to anticipate one odious use which is too commonly made of this despotism, in extorting, from the fears of the young females who are subject to it, compliances with the licentious desires of the drivers, which they might otherwise have refused from attachment to another, if not from moral feelings and restraints. It is idle and insulting to talk of improving the condition of these poor beings, as rational and moral agents, while they are treated in a manner which precludes self-government, and annihilates all human motives but such as we impose on a maniac, or on a hardened and incorrigible convict.

Another abuse which shews, like the rest, the extreme degradation of the Negro race, and the apathy which it creates in their masters, is the cruel, and, at least in the case of the female sex, highly indecent punishments inflicted in public, and in the face of day, often in the presence of the gang, or of the whole assembled population of an estate. From their low and ignominious condition it doubtless proceeds, that they are in some degree regarded as below the necessity of observing towards others the proper decencies of life, or of having those decencies observed by others towards them.

It is no doubt also chiefly owing to their not being yet raised out of that extreme depth in which they are sunk, so much below the level of the human species, that no attempts have been made to introduce among them the Christian institution of marriage, that blessed union which the Almighty himself established as a fundamental law, at the creation of man, to be as it were the well-spring of all the charities of life—the source of all domestic comfort and social improvement,—the moral cement of civilized society.

In truth, so far have the masters been from attempting to establish marriage generally among their slaves, that even the idea of its introduction among them never seems to have seriously suggested itself to their minds. In the commencement of the long contest concerning the abolition of the Slave Trade, it was one of a number of questions respecting the treatment of slaves in the West Indies put by the Privy Council,—"What is the practice respecting the marriage of Negro Slaves, and what are the regulations concerning it?" In all instances, and from every colony, the answers returned were such as these: "They do not marry." "They cohabit by mutual consent," &c. "If by marriage is meant a regular contract and union of one man with one woman, enforced by positive institutions, no such practice exists among the slaves, and they are left entirely free in this respect, &c." . . .

I have dwelt the longer, and insisted the more strongly on the universal want of the marriage institution among the slaves, because, among the multiplied abuses of the West Indian system, it appears to me to be one of the most influential in its immoral and degrading effects. It should, however, be remarked, that though the prevalence of promiscuous intercourse between the male and female slaves is nearly universal, yet mutual and exclusive, though rarely permanent attachments between two individuals of different sexes frequently take place; and as the Africans notoriously have warm affections, the regard is often very strong, so long as it continues. On the mother's side also the instincts of nature are too sure not to produce great affection for her children, some degree of which also will often be found in the father. But how far are these precarious connections from producing that growing attachment, that mutual confidence, which spring from an identity of interest, from the common feeling for a common progeny, with all the multiplied emotions of hope and even of fear, of joys and even of sorrows, which bind families together, when mutually attached to each other by the indissoluble bonds of a Christian union? Alas! the injustice with which these poor creatures are treated accompanies them throughout the whole of their progress; and even the cordial drops which a gracious Providence has elsewhere poured into the cup of poverty and labour, are to them vitiated and embittered.

It must also be observed, that licentiousness thus produced is not confined to the Negroes. The fact is perfectly notorious, that it has been the general policy to employ instead of married managers and overseers, single young men as the immediate superintendents of the gangs; and hence it too naturally follows, that they who, from their being the depositories of the master's authority, ought to be the protectors of the purity of the young females, too often become their corrupters.

It is a farther important truth, pregnant with the most serious consequences, that the extreme degradation which is supposed to render the slaves unfit to form the marriage contract, belongs not merely to their situation as slaves, but to their colour as Negroes. Hence it adheres not only to those who are for ever released from slavery, but to those also who, by having one European parent, might be presumed to be raised highly above the level of the servile race. Such is the incurable infamy inherent in what still belongs to them of African origin, that they are at an almost immeasurable distance in the scale of being below the lowest of the whites.* The free women of colour deem an illicit connection with a white man more respectable than a legal union with a coloured husband. . . .

In my estimate of things, however, and I trust in that of the bulk of my countrymen, though many of the physical evils of our colonial slavery are cruel, and odious, and pernicious, the almost universal destitution of religious and moral instruction among the slaves is the most serious of all the vices of the West Indian system; and had there been no other, this alone would have most powerfully enforced on my conscience the obligation of publicly declaring my decided conviction, that it is the duty of the legislature of this country to interpose for the mitigation and future termination of a state in which the ruin of the moral man, if I may so express myself, has been one of the sad consequences of his bondage.

It cannot be denied, I repeat, that the slaves, more especially the great body of the field Negroes, are practically strangers to the multiplied blessings of the Christian Revelation.

What a consideration is this! A nation, which besides the invaluable benefit of an unequalled degree of true civil liberty, has been favoured with an unprecedented measure of religious light, with its long train of attendant blessings, has been for two centuries detaining in a state of slavery, beyond example rigorous, and in some particulars worse than pagan darkness and depravity, hundreds of thousands of their fellow

---

* The extreme degradation of the coloured race, as it affects their marriage relations, is strikingly illustrated by a passage in one of the many pamphlets published.

creatures, originally torn from their native land by fraud and violence. Generation after generation have thus been pining away; and in this same condition of ignorance and degradation they still, for the most part, remain. This I am well aware is an awful charge; but it undeniably is too well founded, and scarcely admits of any exception beyond what has been effected by those excellent, though too commonly traduced and persecuted men, the Christian missionaries. They have done all that it has been possible for them to do; and through the divine blessing they have indeed done much especially in the towns, and among the household slaves, considering the many and great obstacles with which they have had to contend. . . .

But farther I will frankly confess, that we greatly deceived ourselves by expecting much more benefit to the plantation Negroes from the abolition of the Slave Trade than has actually resulted from that measure. We always relied much on its efficiency in preparing the way for a general emancipation of the slaves: for let it be remembered, that, from the very first, Mr. Pitt, Mr. Fox, Lord Grenville, Lord Lansdowne, Lord Grey, and all the rest of the earliest abolitionists, declared that the extinction of slavery was our great and ultimate object; and we trusted, that by compelling the planters to depend wholly on native increase for the supply of their gangs, they would be forced to improve the condition of their slaves, to increase their food, to lessen their labour, to introduce task-work, to abolish the driving system, together with degrading and indecent punishments, to attach the slaves to the soil, and, with proper qualifications, to admit their testimony as witnesses—a necessary step to all protection by law; above all, to attend to their religious and moral improvement, and to one of the grand peculiarities of Christianity, the marriage institution. By the salutary operation of these various improvements, the slaves would have become qualified for the enjoyment of liberty; and preparation would have been made for that happy day, when the yoke should be taken off for ever, when the blessed transmutation should take place of a degraded slave population into a free and industrious peasantry. . . .

We were too sanguine in our hopes as to the effects of the abolition in our colonies; we judged too favourably of human nature; we thought too well of the colonial assemblies; we did not allow weight enough to the effects of rooted prejudice and inveterate habits—to absenteeship, a vice which, taken in its whole extent, is perhaps one of the most injurious of the whole system; to the distressed finances of the planters; and, above all, to the effects of the extreme degradation of the Negro slaves, and to the long and entire neglect of Christianity among them, with all its attendant blessings.

True it is, that from the want of effectual Register acts, the experiment has not been fairly tried; as the abolition is in consequence known to be a law that may easily be evaded. For, let it be ever borne in mind, that the ground of our persuasion was, that the absolute prohibition of all future importation of slaves into the colonies, provided means were adopted for insuring its permanent execution, would exercise a sort of moral compulsion over the minds of the planters, and even of their managers and overseers, and induce them, for the necessary end of maintaining the black population, to adopt effectual measures for reforming the principal abuses of the system: but it is manifest, that such compulsion could not arise from a law which they had power to elude at pleasure. I am willing, however, for my own part, to admit that this foundation-stone of our hopes may have rested on sandy ground; for what has since passed has proved to me how little prudence and foresight can effect in opposition to the stubborn prejudices, and strong passions, and inveterate habits that prevail in our West Indian assemblies. With one single exception in favour of the free coloured people in Jamaica, the admission of their evidence, which, however, only placed them in the situation which they had always before occupied in most of our other islands, I know not any vice of the system that has been rooted out, any material improvement that has been adopted. . . .

I press these topics the more earnestly, because there has prevailed among many of our statesmen, of late years, a most unwarrantable and pernicious disposition to leave all that concerns the well-being of the slaves to the colonial legislatures. Surely this is a course manifestly contrary to the clearest obligations of duty. The very relation in which the Negro slaves and the members of the colonial assemblies, which consist wholly of their masters, stand towards each other, is of itself a decisive reason why the imperial legislature ought to consider itself bound to exercise the office of an umpire, or rather of a judge between them, as constituting two parties of conflicting interests and feelings. And this, let it be remembered, not merely because, knowing the frailty of our common nature, and its disposition to abuse absolute power, we ought not to deliver the weaker party altogether into the power of the stronger; but because in the present instance there are peculiar objections of great force, some of which have been already noticed. In truth, West Indians must be exempt from the ordinary frailties of human nature, if, living continually with those wretched beings, and witnessing their extreme degradation and consequent depravity, they could entertain for the Negroes, in an unimpaired degree, that equitable consideration and that fellow-feeling, which are due from man to man; so as to sympathise properly with them in their sufferings and wrongs, or form a

just estimate of their claims to personal rights and moral improvement....

Indeed, the West Indians, in the warmth of argument, have gone still
farther, and have even distinctly told us, again and again, and I am
shocked to say that some of their partizans in this country have re-
echoed the assertion, that these poor degraded beings, the Negro slaves,
are as well or even better off than our British peasantry,—a proposition
so monstrous, that nothing can possibly exhibit in a stronger light the
extreme force of the prejudices which must exist in the minds of its
assertors. A Briton to compare the state of a West Indian slave with that
of an English freeman, and to give the former the preference! It is to
imply an utter insensibility of the native feelings and moral dignity
of man, no less than of the rights of Englishmen!! I will not condescend
to argue this question, as I might, on the ground of comparative feeding
and clothing, and lodging, and medical attendance. Are these the only
claims? are these the chief privileges of a rational and immortal being?
Is the consciousness of personal independence nothing? are self-
possession and self-government nothing? Is it of no account that our
persons are inviolate by any private authority, and that the whip is
placed only in the hands of the public executioner; Is it of no value that
we have the power of pursuing the occupation and the habits of life
which we prefer; that we have the prospect, or at least the hope, of
improving our condition, and of rising, as we have seen others rise,
from poverty and obscurity to comfort, and opulence, and distinction?
Again, are all the charities of the heart, which arise out of the domestic
relations, to be considered as nothing; and, I may add, all their security
too among men who are free agents, and not vendible chattels, liable
continually to be torn from their dearest connections, and sent into a
perpetual exile? Are husband and wife, parent and child, terms of no
meaning? Are willing services, or grateful returns for voluntary kind-
nesses, nothing? But, above all, is Christianity so little esteemed among
us, that we are to account as of no value the hope, "full of immortality,"
the light of heavenly truth, and all the consolations and supports by which
religion cheers the hearts and elevates the principles, and dignifies the
conduct of multitudes of our labouring classes in this free and enlightened country? Is it nothing to be taught that all human distinctions
will soon be at an end; that all the labours and sorrows of poverty and
hardship will soon exist no more; and to know, on the express authority
of Scripture, that the lower classes, instead of being an inferior order
in the creation, are even the preferable objects of the love of the
Almighty?

But such wretched sophisms as insult the understandings of mankind, are sometimes best answered by an appeal to their feelings. Let me therefore ask, is there, in the whole of the three kingdoms, a parent or a husband so sordid and insensible that any sum, which the richest West Indian proprietor could offer him, would be deemed a compensation for his suffering his wife or his daughter to be subjected to the brutal outrage of the cart-whip—to the savage lust of the driver—to the indecent, and degrading, and merciless punishment of a West Indian whipping? If there were one so dead, I say not to every liberal, but to every natural feeling, as that money could purchase of him such concessions, such a wretch, and he alone, would be capable of the farther sacrifices necessary for degrading an English peasant to the condition of the West Indian slave. He might consent to sell the liberty of his own children, and to barter away even the blessings conferred on himself by that religion which declares to him that his master, no less than himself, has a Master in heaven—a common Creator, who is no respecter of persons, and in whose presence he may weekly stand on the same spiritual level with his superiors in rank, to be reminded of their common origin, common responsibility, and common day of final and irreversible account. . . .

The same testimony as to the progress of the Negro children, in common school learning, has been given by all the masters who have instructed them in the Island of Hayti; and the missionaries, in our different West Indian islands, testify, with one consent, the gratitude and attachment which the West Indian, no less than the Sierra Leone Negroes feel to those who condescend to become their teachers.

Again, the impression so assiduously attempted heretofore to be made, that the *indolence* of the Negro race was utterly incurable, and that without the driving whip they never would willingly engage in agricultural labour, has been shewn to be utterly without foundation. Mr. Parke relates, that the Africans, when prompted by any adequate motives, would work diligently and perseveringly both in agricultural and manufacturing labours. And there is on the African coast a whole nation of the most muscular men and the hardiest labourers, who, from their known industry, are hired both for government service, and by the European traders, as workmen, both on ship-board and on shore.

Nor have instances of a similar kind been wanting even in the West Indies, whenever circumstances have been at all favourable to voluntary industry. Since the dissolution of the black corps, (a measure which the abolitionists are scarcely, I fear, excusable for not having opposed, though prompted to acquiesce in it by unwillingness to thwart, when not indispensably necessary, the prejudices of the colonists) many of the disbanded soldiers have maintained themselves by their own agricultural labours, and have manifested a degree of industry that ought to have silenced for ever all imputations on the diligence of their race. . . .

But while we are loudly called on by justice and humanity to take measures without delay for improving the condition of our West Indian slaves, self-interest also inculcates the same duty, and with full as clear a voice. It is a great though common error, that notwithstanding we must, on religious and moral grounds, condemn the West Indian system, yet, that in a worldly view, it has been eminently gainful both to individuals and to the community at large. On the contrary, I believe it might be proved to any inquiring and unprejudiced mind, that taking in all considerations of political economy, and looking to the lamentable waste of human life among our soldiers and seamen, raised and recruited at a great expence, as well as to the more direct pecuniary charge of protecting the sugar colonies, no system of civil polity was ever maintained at a greater price, or was less truly profitable either to individuals or to the community, than that of our West Indian settlements. Indeed, it would have been a strange exception to all those established principles which Divine Providence, has ordained for the moral benefit of the world, if national and personal prosperity were generally and permanently to be found to arise from injustice and oppression. There may be individual instances of great fortunes amassed by every species of wrong doing. A course, ruinous in the long run, may, to an individual, or for a time, appear eminently profitable; nevertheless, it is unquestionably true, that the path of prosperity rarely diverges long and widely from that of integrity and virtue; or, to express it in a familiar adage,—that honesty is the best policy. . . .

To the real nature of the West Indian system, and still more to the extent of its manifold abuses, the bulk even of well-informed men in this country are, I believe, generally strangers. May it not be from our having sinned in ignorance that we have so long been spared ? But ignorance of a duty which we have had abundant means of knowing to be such, can by no one be deemed excusable. Let us not presume too far on the forbearance of the Almighty. Favoured in an unequalled degree with Christian light, with civil freedom, and with a greater measure of national blessings than perhaps any other country upon earth ever before enjoyed, what a return would it be for the goodness of the Almighty, if we were to continue to keep the descendants of the Africans, whom we have ourselves wrongfully planted in the western hemisphere, in their present state of unexampled darkness and degradation!

While efforts are making to rescue our country from this guilt and this reproach, let every one remember that he is answerable for any measure of assistance which Providence has enabled him to render towards the accomplishment of the good work. In a country in which the popular voice has a powerful and constitutional influence on the government and legislation, to be silent when there is a question of reforming abuses repugnant to justice and humanity, is to share their guilt. Power always implies responsibility; and the possessor of it cannot innocently be neutral when by his exertion moral good may be promoted, or evil lessened or removed.

If I may presume to employ a few words on what belongs more particularly to the writer of these lines, I can truly declare, that an irresistible conviction that it is his positive duty to endeavour to rouse his countrymen to a just sense of the importance and urgency of our duties towards the Negro Slaves, has alone compelled him reluctantly thus to come forward again in such an arduous cause as this, and at a period of life when nature shrinks from a laborious contest. He can but too surely anticipate from experience, that the grossest and most unfounded calumnies will be profusely poured out against him; but he nevertheless proceeds, animated by the wish, and, he will add, the confident hope, that the cause of our African brethren will deeply interest the public mind, and that the legislature will be induced to adopt the course prescribed to us by the strongest obligations of moral and religious duty.

Before I conclude, may I presume to interpose a word of caution to my fellow-labourers in this great cause,—a caution which I can truly say I have ever wished myself to keep in remembrance, and observe in practice: it is, that while we expose and condemn the evils of the system itself, we should treat with candour and tenderness the characters of the West Indian proprietors. Let not the friends of the Africans forget that they themselves might have inherited West Indian property; and that by early example and habit they might have been subjected to the very prejudices which they now condemn. I have before declared, and I now willingly repeat, that I sincerely believe many of the owners of West Indian estates to be men of more than common kindness and liberality; but I myself have found many of them, as I have had every reason to believe, utterly unacquainted with the true nature and practical character of the system with which they have the misfortune to be connected.

While, however, we speak and act towards the colonists personally with fair consideration and becoming candour, let our exertions in the cause of the unfortunate slaves be zealous and unremitting. Let us act with an energy suited to the importance of the interests for which we contend. Justice, humanity, and sound policy prescribe our course, and will animate our efforts. Stimulated by a consciousness of what we owe to the laws of God and the rights and happiness of man, our exertions will be ardent, and our perseverance invincible. Our ultimate success is sure; and ere long we shall rejoice in the consciousness of having delivered our country from the greatest of her crimes, and rescued her character from the deepest stain of dishonour.

2. *A Brief View of the Nature and Effects of Negro Slavery As It Exists in the Colonies of Great Britain* (London, 1830)

18, ALDERMANBURY,
October 1, 1830.

The Committee of the SOCIETY FOR THE ABOLITION OF SLAVERY THROUGHOUT THE BRITISH DOMINIONS, understanding that a strong and very general desire prevails, in all parts of the country, to be furnished with a compendious view of the Nature and Effects of Negro Slavery, as it exists in the Colonies of Great Britain, have thought it their duty to draw up and circulate the following summary of information on that subject:—

THE Slave Colonies are divided into two classes; one called Crown Colonies, subject to the legislation of the Crown, and containing 225,000 Slaves; the other Chartered Colonies, having legislatures of their own, and containing about 580,000 Slaves.

In these Colonies, therefore, of Great Britain, there are at this moment upwards of 800,000 human beings in a state of degrading personal slavery.

These unhappy persons, whether young or old, male or female, are the absolute property of their master, who may sell or transfer them at his pleasure, and who may also regulate according to his discretion (within certain limits,) the measure of their labour, their food, and their punishment.

Many of the Slaves are (and all may be) branded like cattle, by means of a hot iron, on the shoulder or other conspicuous part of the body, with the initials of their master's name: and thus bear about them, in indelible characters, the proof of their debased and servile state.

The Slaves, whether male or female, are forced to labour, for the sole benefit of their owners, from whom they receive no wages; and this labour is continued (with certain intermissions for breakfast and dinner,) from morning to night, throughout the year.

In the season of crop, which lasts for four or five months of the year, their labour is protracted not only throughout the day, as at other times, but during either half the night, or the whole of every alternate night.

Thus their daily average labour throughout the year amounts to the enormous rate of fifteen or sixteen hours a day.

Besides being generally forced to work without wages, and in the Chartered Colonies under the immediate impulse of the lash, most of the Slaves are further obliged to labour for their own maintenance on that day which ought to be devoted to repose and religious instruction. And as that day is also their only market day, it follows, that "Sunday shines no Sabbath-day to them," but is of necessity a day of worldly occupation, and much bodily exertion.

The Colonial Laws arm the master, or any one to whom he may delegate his authority, with a power to punish his Slaves to a certain extent, without the intervention of the magistrate, and without any responsibility for the use of this tremendous discretion; and to that extent he may punish them for any offence, or for no offence. These discretionary punishments are usually inflicted on the naked body with the cart-whip, an instrument of dreadful severity, which cruelly lacerates the flesh of the sufferer. Even the unhappy females are still, in all the Chartered Colonies, equally liable with the men to have their persons thus shamelessly exposed and barbarously tortured at the caprice of their master or overseer. In the *Crown* Colonies the flogging of females has been forbidden, as well as the use of the driving whip in the field.

The Slaves being regarded in the eye of the law as mere chattels, they are liable to be seized in execution for their master's debts, and in the Chartered Colonies, without any regard to the family ties which may be broken by this oppressive and merciless process, to be sold by auction to the highest bidder, who may remove them to a distant part of the same colony.

Marriage, that blessing of civilized and even of savage life, had, till lately, no legal sanction in any of the Colonies. It could not therefore be said to exist among the Slaves at all; while those living together as man and wife were liable to be separated by the caprice of their master, or by sale for the satisfaction of his creditors. Marriage is now legalized in the Crown Colonies; but in the Chartered Colonies, though pretending to legalize it, it is still discouraged rather than promoted. In none of the Colonies does it prevail practically to any extent.

The Slaves in general have little or no access to the means of Christian instruction.

The effect of the want of such instruction, as well as the general absence of the marriage tie, is, that the most unrestrained licentiousness (exhibited in a degrading, disgusting and depopulating promiscuous intercourse,) prevails almost universally among the Slaves; and is encouraged no less universally, by the example of their superiors the Whites.

The evidence of Slaves is now admitted in the Crown Colonies; but with two exceptions, it is not admitted in the Chartered Colonies, in any civil or criminal case affecting a person of free condition. If a White man, therefore, perpetrates the most atrocious acts of barbarity, in the presence of slaves only, the injured party is left without any means of legal redress.

In none of the Chartered Colonies of Great Britain have those legal facilities been afforded to the Slave to purchase his own freedom, which have produced such extensively beneficial effects in the colonial posses-sions of Spain and Portugal; where the Slaves have been manumitted in large numbers, not only without injury, but with benefit to the master, and with decided advantage to the public peace and safety. In the Crown Colonies, some considerable facilities to manumission have recently been afforded.

It is a general principle of Colonial Law, that all Black or Coloured persons are presumed and taken to be Slaves, unless they can legally prove the contrary. The liberty, therefore, even of free persons is thus often greatly endangered, and sometimes lost. They are liable to be apprehended as run-away Slaves; and they are further liable, as such, to be sold into endless bondage, if they fail to do that which, though free, nay, though born perhaps in Great Britain itself, they may be unable to do—namely, to establish the fact of their freedom by such evidence as the colonial laws require.

Let it be remembered also, that many thousand infants are annually born within the British dominions to no inheritance but that of the hapless, hopeless servitude which has been described; and the general oppressiveness of which might be inferred from this striking and most opprobrious fact alone, that while in the West Indies the Free Blacks and People of Colour multiply rapidly, and in the United States of American even the Slaves increase so fast as to double their number in twenty years—there is, even now, in the British colonies, no increase, but on the contrary a diminution of their numbers.

Such are some of the more prominent features of Negro Slavery, as it exists in the Colonies of Great Britain. Revolting as they are, they form only a part of those circumstances of wretchedness and degradation which might be pointed out as characterizing that unhappy state of being.

Confining, however, our view to the particulars which have been specified, every enlightened Christian, nay, every reasonable man, must allow that it is a case which calls loudly for interference. Is it possible that any free-born Briton should contemplate such a state of things without the liveliest emotions of shame and grief and indignation; or that, satisfied with the recollection of his own comforts, he should refuse to listen to the cry of the wretched Negro? These things being made known to us, we are bound, without hesitation or delay, to come forward and address our earnest petitions to the Legislature, that a remedy may be applied to such enormous evils, and that our country may be delivered from the guilt of participating in a system so fraught with the grossest injustice and oppression to hundreds of thousands of our fellow-subjects.

It will hardly be alleged, that any man can have a RIGHT to retain his fellow-creatures in a state so miserable and degrading as has been described. And the absence of such RIGHT will be still more apparent, if we consider how these Slaves were originally obtained. They, or their parents, were the victims of the Slave Trade. They were obtained, not by any lawful means, or under any colourable pretext, but by the most undisguised rapine and the most atrocious fraud. Torn from their homes and from every dear relation in life, barbarously manacled, driven like herds of cattle to the sea shore, crowded into the pestilential holds of slave ships, they were transported to our colonies, and there sold into interminable bondage.

Great Britain, it is true, has abolished her African Slave Trade, and branded it as felony; and it is impossible to reflect without exultation on that great act of national justice.

The grateful acknowledgments of the country are also due to the Government, for their persevering efforts to induce other nations to follow the same course, and thus to rescue Africa from the desolating effects of the Slave Trade. Those efforts, though hitherto unattended with all the success they merit, it is hoped, will be strenuously and unremittingly continued, until that nefarious traffic shall be declared PIRACY by the concurrent voice of all nations.

When the British Slave Trade was abolished, a confident expectation was entertained that the certain result of that measure would be the rapid mitigation and final extinction of the colonial bondage which had sprung from it, and which in its principle is equally indefensible.

Twenty-three years, however, have now elapsed since the British Slave Trade was abolished; but, during that long period, what effectual steps have been taken, either in this country or in the colonies, for mitigating the rigours of Negro bondage, or for putting an end to a condition of society which so grievously outrages every feeling of humanity, while it violates every recognised principle both of the British Constitution and of the Christian religion?

The Government and Legislature of this country have, on various occasions, and in the most solemn and unequivocal terms, denounced

the Slave Trade as immoral, inhuman, and unjust; but the legal per-
petuation of that state of Slavery, which has been produced by it, is
surely in its principle, no less immoral, inhuman, and unjust, than the
trade itself.

Notwithstanding these solemn denunciations, thousands of children
are still annually born SLAVES within the British dominions, and
upwards of 800,000 of our fellow-creatures (the victims of the Slave
Trade, or descended from its victims,) are still retained in the same state
of brutal depression. They are still driven like cattle to their uncom-
pensated toil by the impulse of the lash. They are still exposed to severe
and arbitrary punishments. They are still bought and sold as merchan-
dise. They are still without the blessings of the marriage tie, and of the
Christian Sabbath. And, in a variety of other respects, they continue
to be an oppressed and degraded race, wholly excluded from the civil
privileges, and without any adequate participation in the religious
advantages, to which, as British subjects, they are unquestionably
entitled.

It is not intended to attribute the existence and continuance of this
most opprobrious system to our Colonies exclusively. The guilt and
shame arising from it belong in perhaps an equal degree, certainly in a
great degree, to the People and Parliament of this country. But on that
very account we are the more rigidly bound to lose no time in adopting
such measures as shall bring this state of cruel bondage to the earliest
termination which is compatible with the well-being of the parties who
sustain its grievous yoke.

But, besides our paramount and indispensable obligations, on moral
and religious grounds, to relieve our colonial bondsmen from the cruel
and degrading condition to which we have reduced them, and to remedy
as far as we can the numberless wrongs of which we have been the
criminal authors; it is further due to the character of Great Britain, in
the eyes of foreign nations, that we should act agreeably to the principles
which, in our discussions with them relative to the African Slave
Trade, we have professed to make the basis of our representations.
It would be vain to expect that they should regard those professions as
otherwise than insincere, or that they should defer to our representations,
however urgent, if we exhibit in our own conduct the glaring incon-
sistency of sanctioning as legal, in our own dominions, practices of the
very same nature, in effect, with those which we reprobate and denounce
as immoral, inhuman, and unjust, when they occur on the coast of
Africa.

It is therefore our clear and indisputable duty completely to reform
our present colonial system, even if it should require a large pecuniary

sacrifice to accomplish that object. But the proposed change, we believe, is prescribed to us not more by moral and religious principle, than by the soundest views of political expediency. In the present advanced state of knowledge, it can no longer be a question that the labour of slaves is much less profitable than that of freemen, and that it can only be supported at a very heavy expense to the community at large. In proof of this, it will be sufficient to adduce the protecting duties and bounties afforded to the growers of sugar in the West Indies; and without which they declare it would be impossible for them to continue its culture. Indeed, we are persuaded that no institution which is directly at variance with the will of the Supreme Governor of the Universe can prove a source of permanent advantage either to nations or individuals. And, in the present case, it might be clearly demonstrated, that the personal slavery which deforms the face of society in the British colonies, and stains the British character, is as detrimental to the interests of the Slave owner as it is cruel and oppressive to the Slave; and that its abolition, instead of proving an injury to either, will prove an unspeakable benefit to both.

The Colonists say, that they shall sustain a great actual loss by the proposed change of system. If so, they will of course have an opportunity of preferring and establishing their claim to indemnity. But, whatever the extent of that claim may be proved to be, it is obvious that it attaches not to the Negro bondsman, but to the British nation. It would be repugnant to every idea of equity, if we were to discharge any debt we may owe to the Colonists, not from our own resources, but with the toil and sweat and blood of our African brethren.

But, in whatever degree it may be found necessary to indemnify the Colonists for any loss which may arise to them from the abolition of Negro Slavery, yet, *while that state of society continues unchanged*, there will be an insuperable objection in the mind of every conscientious individual to the adoption of any measures of pecuniary relief, by means of protecting duties or bounties on their produce or otherwise; because it is obvious that such measures, however modified, would involve the people of this country in the farther guilt of upholding a system which, when the facts of the case are known, it is impossible not to feel to be utterly repugnant to the principles of justice and humanity, and to the whole spirit of Christianity.

In any event, it is hoped that this momentous subject will be taken into the earliest consideration of Parliament, with the view of providing an effectual remedy for the evils of colonial bondage, and raising the unhappy subjects of it from their present state of wretchedness and degradation, to the enjoyment of the blessings of civil freedom and religious light; and it appears the unquestionable duty of the friends of humanity, in all parts of the kingdom, to address their early and earnest petitions to the Legislature for that purpose.

Donations or Annual Subscriptions, in aid of the Society's object, are received by the Treasurer, SAMUEL HOARE, Esq. 62, Lombard Street;— by the Secretary, THOMAS PRINGLE, Esq. (to whom communications may be addressed,) 18, Aldermanbury;—by Messrs. HATCHARD, 187, Piccadilly, and Messrs. ARCH, Cornhill, Booksellers to the Society;— and by the following Bankers, viz. Messrs. HOARE, Fleet Street; and and Messrs. DRUMMOND, Charing Cross.

3. FROM *Memoirs of Sir Thomas Fowell Buxton, Baronet, with Selections From His Correspondence,* edited by Charles Buxton (American edition, Philadelphia, 1849)

The new Parliament, which had met on the 14th of June, was altogether occupied in debates on the Reform Bill, and Mr. Buxton, who was deeply interested in the progress of the measure, was detained in London till September.

The following paper was written after his return to his usual recreations in the country.

Northrepps Hall, October 26, 1831.

"Samuel Hoare goes away to-day. Shooting has been good medicine for him; he came down with very gloomy views on the state of public affairs,—but the dangers from Reform or the rejection of Reform—the perils of the Church and the State, have gradually disappeared, and now, as far as he can see, the country, if not prosperous and secure, is at least threatened with no imminent danger! As for myself, I feel about shooting, that it is not time lost if it contributes to my health and cheerfulness. I have many burdens, and it is well to cast them off, lest they should so dispirit and oppress me, that I become less capable of active exertion.

"But now my holiday is nearly ended; shooting may be my recreation, but it is not my business. It has pleased God to place some duties upon me with regard to the poor slaves, and those duties I must not abandon. Oppression, and cruelty, and persecution, and, what is worse, absence of religion, must not continue to grind that unfortunate race through my neglect. Grant, O God! that I may be enabled by thy Holy Spirit to discharge my solemn duties to them. Thou hast promised thy Spirit, thy aid, and thy wisdom to those who ask them, and under a sense of my utter incompetency to do any thing of my own strength, I humbly and earnestly crave and entreat thy guiding wisdom, and that power and strength which cometh from thee. Make me an instrument in thy hands for the relief, and for the elevation of that afflicted people. For the oppression of the poor, for the sighing of the needy, now arise, O Lord! and grant me the privilege of labouring, and combating in their behalf. . . . . . . Once more I pray that it may please thee, O God! for Christ's sake, to lift up the light of thy countenance on me, my labours, my meditations, and my prayers; grant me to grow in grace, and call forth the powers thou hast given me for thy own service; strengthen me with might in the inner man; deal bountifully with thy servant. Amen."

. . . truth, have been to me abundant and innumerable, as the leaves of the forest, as the sands of the sea. Benignant and bountiful hast thou been to me all the days of my life, and may it please thee evermore to be so, to continue to bless me in body, in mind, in estate, in pursuits, in family, in friends, in business, in prayer, in meditation, in thankfulness for the visible mercy of God, and in the atonement of Christ.

. . . .

"We stand now in a peculiar crisis; though I am not troubled with care, or depressed with apprehension, there is reason for alarm. It is both in private and public matters, a time of trouble, and I have good reason to seek thee with earnestness of supplication in this perilous period. As for public matters, have I not reason to turn steadfastly to Him who can shield us from dangers, however imminent and however terrible? Last week the Bristol riots prevailed, and the same spirit may spread through the country. In this neighbourhood the incendiary has been briskly at work. Last night the news arrived that the cholera had really commenced its ravages in England; and to-morrow a meeting of the working classes is to take place in London. Storms seem gathering in every direction, and the tempest may soon break upon my own house. Assist me, then, O Lord! to prepare for events which may so soon approach. Let my house be planted on a rock which shall stand firm in the buffetings of the winds and the waves. Oh my God! I feel that there is no security, save the perfect security which belongs to thee. Vain is the help of man; folly is his wisdom; feebleness is his strength; but in entire unshaken confidence I desire to commit and to commend to thee myself, my family, my friends, my neighbours, my country.

"Give us wisdom to act aright; preside over our councils; lead us to the right path, and to do to the right thing. Let thy Spirit be poured forth upon us in rich profusion, prepare us for outward danger by inward grace. Teach us that no real calamity can befall us if we are in the hands of our God, that we are safe under the shadow of his wings. Give us the spirit of true prayer and let it abide with us, and, if death be coming, 'in the hour of death and in the day of judgment, good Lord, deliver us,' for the sake of our blessed Redeemer, Christ Jesus." . . .

"My hope and wish for you is, that you may be led to pray fervently and constantly for the Spirit of God to teach you. If you ask for that Spirit, it will be given to you: it will teach you to read the Bible, it will enlighten your mind on the truths which it contains, and, especially, it will make you to know and feel two things,—first, that God is ready to pardon even the greatest of sinners; and, secondly, that this pardon is derived, not from our own merits, but from the merits of our Saviour.

"I have been led, my dear friend, to say thus much from the sincere interest and friendship I have always felt for you. I entreat you to take it as kindly as it is meant, and to make good use of the leisure, which you now have, in attending to the most important concern you ever were engaged in."

The following is an extract from one of his papers, dated Jan. 1, 1832.

"Grant, O Lord, that I may begin the next year under the guidance and influence of that blessed Spirit, which, if I grieve it not, if I follow it implicitly, if I listen to its still small voice, if I love it as my friend and consult it as my counsellor, will surely lead me in this life, in the pleasant paths of peace and holiness, and as surely conduct me hereafter to the habitations of unutterable joy.

"Again and again I crave and entreat the presence and the power of that heavenly guide. O Lord, how much have I had in the past year to thank thee for! What mercy, what love, what compassion for my weakness, what readiness to pardon and obliterate the memory of my misdeeds. . . .

"Now am I sufficiently assiduous in the discharge of my duties? My great duty is the deliverance of my brethren in the West Indies from slavery both of body and soul. In the early part of the year I did in some measure faithfully discharge this. I gave my whole mind to it. I remember that I prayed for firmness and resolution to persevere, and that in spite of some formidable obstructions I was enabled to go on; but, latterly, where has my heart been? Has the bondage of my brethren engrossed my whole mind? The plain and the painful truth is that it has not. Pardon, O Lord, this neglect of this honourable service to which thou hast called me.

"Give me wisdom to devise, and ability to execute, and zeal and perseverance and dedication of heart, for the task with which thou hast been pleased to honour me. 2 Chron. xx. 12—17.

"And now, Lord, hear and answer my prayer for myself; my first desire is, that this next year may not be thrown away upon any thing less than those hopes and interests, which are greater and better than any that this world can contain. May no subordinate cares or earthly interests interrupt my progress. May I act as one whose aim is heaven;

may my loins be girded, and my lights burning, and myself like unto men who wait for their Lord. Conscious of my own weakness, of my absolute inability to do any thing by my own strength, any thing tending to my own salvation, I earnestly pray for the light and the impulse of thy Holy Spirit, and that Christ may dwell in my heart by faith.

"Bless, O Lord God, my efforts for the extinction of that cruel slavery; or, rather, take the work into thine own hands.

"Bless, O Lord, I earnestly pray thee, bless my family, relations and friends. With what deep affection I pass them in review, and feel that never was any one privileged to possess a larger number of most faithful friends. I entreat, O Lord, that thou wouldest bless them with all thy choicest blessings, in their families, in their concerns, in their health, and, above all, in the growth of grace in their souls.

"There are some of them from whom I have received much more in kindness than I have ever requited. There are others who seem to need especial intercession. There are those with whom I have all my life been bound by the fastest ties of unclouded affection. For each and for all of them I pray thee, O Lord, turn their hearts to thyself; deliver them from pain, from sorrow, and from sin, and conduct them in thine own way to that fold of which Jesus Christ is the shepherd, and receive them at length as thine own, for the sake of Christ Jesus."

One of his nephews had joined in a school outbreak. Mr. Buxton thus writes to his father—

"Northrepps, January 8, 1832.

"Your letter reached me to-night, and I lose no time in answering it.

"As for the *'insurrectionary movements,'* if you did not take them so seriously, we should rather be inclined to smile at them. Let me ask you one plain question. Do you really think one bit the worse of the boy for having been one of these rebels? I do not. Non-resistance to oppression, or supposed oppression, built upon a deep investigation of the tenor of Scripture, and upon the spirit evinced by the author of Christianity, is a very high attainment: it is not to be expected from a lad of his age. Again, it is of all things the most difficult to stand against the current of popular feeling, especially where the motive for doing so may be misconstrued into timidity and truckling.

"In short, if I were his father, I should affectionately and gently remind him, that his fault consisted in a departure from the principles which his parents held. I should instil into his mind, that it was more noble to stand alone, maintaining that course which they would approve, than to perform the most gallant insurgent exploits; and I should give him to understand that I expected to hear no more of such proceedings: and, in my own heart, I should be quite at ease on the subject. I certainly should send him back again. I would give the school another trial, and I should whisper in the master's ear, that if another rebellion took place, *it must be the fault of the system.*

"The only thing about which I should feel any serious apprehension, should be lest the boy should get indirect praise for his high spirit. I speak from experience. When I was a boy, I obtained what then appeared to me to be the glorious discredit of being high-spirited and haughty, and careless of consequences. There is something in this to please the fancy and excite the pride of a boy; and this character, which stands upon the borders of good and evil, made me very fierce and tyrannical. I say this the more freely, because I think I discern in his mother's letters a great deal of sorrow and apprehension at top, but underneath a little secret, sly satisfaction at her boy's spirit. I send him my love and a sovereign; and, of you like, you may read him what I say, as to the more noble and manly part which we expect him hereafter to take."

. . . .

T. F. Buxton, Esq., to Zachary Macaulay, Esq.

"August 20, 1833.

"My dear Friend,

"Priscilla will tell you what was done last night in the Lords' Committee. The result was, that after two or three rather mischievous alterations, the report passed. The Government told me that the Tories had collected their strength, and were determined to throw out the bill. No symptoms, however, of such infatuation appeared. So now we are nearly at the end of our labours. I must confess I am, if not quite satisfied, exceedingly well pleased. I look back to the letter which you and I wrote to Lord Bathurst in 1823, containing our demands, twelve in number. Bad as the bill is, it accomplishes every one of these, and a great deal more. Among the rest, the day is fixed after which slavery shall not be!

. . . .

"Surely you have reason to rejoice. My sober and deliberate opinion is, that you have done more towards this consummation than any other man. For myself, I take pleasure in acknowledging that you have been my tutor all the way through, and that I could have done nothing without you. . . . . . . This should and must cheer you. It has pleased Providence

to send you sore afflictions, but hundreds of thousands of human beings
will have reason here and hereafter to thank God that your zeal never
slackened, and that you were enabled to labour on against difficulties
and obstacles, of which no one, perhaps, except myself, knew the extent;
dragging to light one abomination after another, till the moral and
religious feeling of the country would endure such crimes no longer.
So cheer up.

"I continue very well. This session has done me less mischief than
any former one. We have had something to console us, and we knew but
very little of that kind of fare in former times.

"Ever yours very truly,
"T. FOWELL BUXTON."

4. FROM *Report of the Agency Committee of the Anti-Slavery Society* (London, 1832)

THE gentlemen to whom the duty of managing the Agency department of the Anti-Slavery Society has been intrusted, have great pleasure in reporting to the Subscribers to this object, that very beneficial results have followed the adoption of the system.

It is expedient briefly to advert to those circumstances in which it originated.

Towards the end of 1830, an unusual degree of excitement upon the question of Negro Slavery obviously pervaded the public mind, and it naturally followed that a spirit of inquiry was awakened; some gentlemen, known to entertain a lively interest on the subject, exerted themselves both in private and public to disseminate the information which they possessed, and this led to a conviction that, although the community appreciated and reprobated as it deserves, "Slavery in the abstract," the peculiar and revolting features of Colonial Slavery were substantially unknown. In a limited circle, consisting of those who had studied the subject as an important legislative question, and of others who from personal observation of the horrors of Slavery had long been active abolitionists, the most accurate and extensive information obtained; but every channel by which such information could be conveyed to the public was closed, either by the prejudices of self interest or by the lavish expenditure of Colonial money. Scarcely a newspaper or a magazine could be found which on this topic was just enough to be neutral, and by far the greater number combined to oppose the abolitionists, whatever might be the distinction of their party or the tenor of their politics. It was mentioned by the editor of a provincial paper, to one of the Agency Committee, that not less than seventy-five guineas had been paid by the Colonial Party to a London newspaper, for the insertion of a single article!

It was a problem of no ordinary difficulty, in what manner to obtain access to the ear of the British Public; for it was well understood by the planters, and experience now daily proves that they were right, that it was only necessary to lay before the country an authentic statement of facts, and all England would rise to demand instant emancipation.

Without any preconcerted arrangement, many gentlemen of acknowledged character and talents spontaneously came forward, in the beginning of last year, to bear an active part in this important controversy. They attended public meetings; in many places the clergy lent their pulpits to the cause, and they found with mingled surprise and regret, that with scarcely any exception, all their auditors now heard for the *first* time facts with which it was supposed, by those who had been studying them for half a century, that the British public must be nearly as familiar as themselves.

The beneficial effect of these exertions was soon perceived by many observing friends of the cause, at a distance from the metropolis. A plan was formed for continuing them by means of lectures to be delivered by stipendiary agents, specially retained for this purpose, and one benevolent lady immediately offered the munificent donation of £100 to carry the plan into operation. This gave encouragement to its projectors to proceed, and the liberal patronage which it has received will be seen in the annexed list of subscriptions. A committee of gentlemen, whose names appear in the title page, was immediately formed to consider the plan in detail, and to direct its progress.

Their first duty was the selection of competent parties to become lecturers, and they rejoice to have it in their power to report, that those gentlemen have well satisfied the expectations which were formed of them: the services which they have rendered will find a more worthy recompense in the approbation of their own consciences, than in the applause of their employers, though sincerely bestowed: their names are, the Rev. E. DEWDNEY, Rev. J. THORP, EDWARD BALDWIN, Esq. GEORGE THOMPSON , Esq.*

Captain CHARLES STUART, E.I.C.E. who is already well known as a persevering, uncompromising friend of the cause, with his accustomed liberality, has also given his gratuitous services, accepting no other return than his travelling expenses, and even those on the most economical scale.

The next duty was of importance scarcely inferior to the judicious selection of agents—to decide upon the instructions which were to guide them in the discharge of their important functions. It was deemed important, at the outset, openly and honestly to avow the principles and to declare the objects of your Committee, and to do so with a precision and sincerity which should set at defiance all the misrepresentations by which the proceedings of the abolitionists have too often been impeded. Such was the feeling of those who were intrusted with the application of this special fund, and, acting upon that feeling, they

---

* The appointment of Mr. Clarkson was only temporary.

prepared the following letter of instructions to their agents, and issued it by authority, in the name of the Parent Committee.

LETTER OF INSTRUCTIONS.

"SIR,—Before the Committee of the Anti-Slavery Society avail themselves of your services as an Agent, it is expedient for them, and but justice to you, that you should be distinctly informed, not only of the nature of the duty which you will have to discharge, but of the principle by which you must be governed, in advocating the abolition of Colonial Slavery; for it is probable that cases may occur, in which it will not be possible to obtain specific instructions from the Committee, and where your judgment must be guided by reference to principle alone, *This principle must be*,—'that the system of Colonial Slavery is a crime in the sight of God, and ought to be immediately and for ever abolished.' If in your opinion the first part of this proposition remains doubtful, it is scarcely necessary to add, that your services will not be accepted by the Committee; but though it would appear that the latter clause must follow as a corollary from the first, it seems expedient to state what is meant by the words 'immediate abolition.'

"It has been frequently urged by the opponents of this cause, that immediate emancipation of the slave would lead to the most calamitous consequences to himself as well as to his master; and this argument has been pressed with great zeal, because it is well calculated to alarm the minds of benevolent individuals, among whom are to be found the most active friends of the Society.

"If by 'immediate emancipation' it were intended to release the slaves from every legal restraint, and that too on the very first day on which intelligence of the measure would be received in our colonies, it might lead to disturbance and extreme distress; but this *never was contemplated* by the Anti-Slavery Society. It admirably suits the policy of its enemies to give this colour to its proceedings; but there is a broad line of demarcation to be drawn between emancipation from all control, at once unlimited in its character and instant in its execution, and an immediate substitution of *judicial* for *private and irresponsible authority*, involving the simultaneous establishment of a system of equality with the free-born subject in the enjoyment of civil rights. *This*, however, is what the Anti-Slavery Society intends by 'immediately abolition;' and if after this explanation, you are not satisfied with the whole proposition that has been laid down as a fundamental principle, it is not probable that your agency will be attended with benefit to the Society or satisfaction to yourself.

"Assuming, however, that you are disposed fully to adopt this principle, the further instructions which the Committee have to give will refer to matters of subordinate importance, in which a greater latitude of discretion can with propriety be allowed; but even here it seems proper to premise, that in the public discussion of the subject, it is the wish of the Committee that you should wholly abstain from any unnecessary introduction of political feeling. The Committee consider this to be a question essentially of a religious character, and though in some degree mixed up on the one hand with matters of political economy, and on the other with the liberty of the subject, it is important not to abandon the high ground of Christian duty, for the sake of gaining the support of a party, or exacting the applause of a popular assembly.

"It is the chief object of the Committee at the present crisis, to prepare the way for a general expression of the public feeling when the time shall arrive, by widely disseminating an accurate knowledge of the nature and effects of Colonial Slavery; and this will be the principal duty you will be called upon to discharge; either by the delivery of lectures upon the subject, or taking a share in the proceedings of a Public Meeting, in places where the local friends of the Society find it convenient to collect one.

"The Committee have no wish to prescribe the form of the proposed address; but it is well to offer a few suggestions as to the arrangement and the substance of it.

"In the first place it is obviously desirable that it should be delivered extempore, and not merely read from paper; nor will this be a matter of much difficulty even with those who are unaccustomed to public speaking, if they avail themselves of some of the many works that have recently been published upon the subject. The Committee would particularly recommend to you an attentive perusal of Godwin's *Lectures*, Stephen's *Delineation of Slavery*, and the *Anti-Slavery Reporter*; in the first, you will find a general but accurate and well written sketch of the whole subject, prepared in the very form which it seems proper for the agents generally to adopt. The second work most ably and completely unveils the Colonial System, by aid of the irresistible evidence of the planters themselves. The *Anti-Slavery Reporter* is a work with which you cannot be too familiar, and which you cannot too carefully consult. It is so copious in its details, so clear in its statements, and so invulnerable in the accuracy of its facts—it abounds with so much, both of solid argument and virtuous indignation, against this system of Colonial oppression, that the Committee cannot too earnestly recommend it to your study; and they are convinced that the advocate who will make himself master of the contents of that publication, can never be at a loss either for arguments, or for documents to support them.

"Another suggestion of great importance is that you should be prepared upon all occasions to substantiate the facts which occur to you to mention, by immediate reference to the authority on which they are stated; and this reference ought not to be merely to the works which have been mentioned, but to the authority which you will find *there* quoted.

"Again, it should be always borne in mind that while particular cases of cruelty or oppression, tending to throw light on Colonial Slavery, are useful to illustrate the system, and to prove that it cannot exist without such cases being of frequent occurrence, it is not expedient to bring them forward in a manner that implies exclusive reliance upon them for support to the cause of abolition; far more useful though perhaps less interesting arguments are to be derived from the statistics of every Colony; and the general principles of religious duty and commercial policy give a more solid foundation for appeals to the public judgment.

"In the intervals which will necessarily elapse between your lectures, it is requested that you will exert yourself to obtain every information in your power respecting the feeling that prevails in the neighbourhood in favour of the cause; and especially that you will inquire what individuals reside there among the influential classes of society, who are likely to lend it their assistance, in the event of a new election, or of an appeal to Parliament. You will have the goodness to transmit from time to time to the Committee, the names and addresses of such persons, accompanied by any information you may acquire, as to the degree of influence which they possess, and the direction in which it could be exerted.

"The Committee have further to suggest, that no exertion should be spared to prevail on the editors of the provincial papers, not only to report the substance of your lecture, or the proceedings of your Public Meeting, but if possible to lend their columns generally to the introduction of Anti-Slavery articles, and to make their own comments upon the subject. This duty must be discharged with great discretion.

"In conclusion, you will bear in mind, that the Committee, while they deem it their duty to awaken public attention to the evils of Colonial Slavery, deprecate all methods of doing so which will not bear the most rigid examination. You will remember, that it is your task to advocate Christian principles in a Christian spirit. You will avoid then, all exaggeration; all intemperance; all party spirit, and personal vituperation. These weapons, unworthy of the holy cause you plead, would be calculated to impede its advancement. An appeal to facts rather than declamation, to the judgment rather than the passions of the nation; an honest, clear, and earnest exposure of the wrongs and woes of our Negro brethren, will accomplish that which the Committee alone design, the dissemination of the truth. And they doubt not that when the truth is known, the nation will view the system of Colonial Slavery in its proper light.

"Should any unexpected difficulty arise which seems to require the advice of the Committee, you will of course immediately communicate with the Secretary; but you cannot err materially, if you take for your guide the principle already given to you, that this system is a crime in the sight of God, and that you are employed as the agent of a Society that seeks on Christian principles its immediate abolition.

"I remain, &c."

The Committee appeal with confidence to the liberality of those friends of the cause who have not hitherto subscribed to this special fund, to come forward in its support, and to solicit the contributions of their neighbours and connections: but a very small portion of England has yet been visited, and Ireland, Scotland, and Wales have been left altogether untouched. Even as respects those places where the agents have already lectured, it would be extremely desirable to repeat the lecture, and it is clear that large and respectable audiences attend with readiness: unless, however, the resources of the Committee are considerably reinforced, it will be impracticable to extend its operations, or even to continue them except upon a very limited scale; for it will be seen by the annexed account that though every thing has been done in the most economical manner, the finances of the Committee are nearly exhausted. The Committee would particularly urge these considerations on those public and acknowledged friends of the Anti-Slavery cause, the absence of whose names from the present list of subscriptions can only be attributed to a distrust of the practicability of the scheme, which must be now removed from every candid mind; for large as the sum subscribed appears to be, let it be observed that there are only twenty-five individuals in the extensive list of Anti-Slavery friends who have contributed to raise it!!! The Committee have received several offers, especially from Dissenting Ministers, to lecture gratuitously in their respective neighbourhoods. They feel grateful for the valuable assistance thus afforded, and so long as a strict adherence is given to the principles of their Letter of Instructions to the stipendiary agents, the Committee will consider themselves bound to give every assistance in their power to gratuitous advocates of the cause.

In conclusion the Committee feel it right to express their conviction that the encouraging proofs which have been given of success are, under God, to be attributed to an open avowal of Christian principles, and an unqualified declaration of the specific object which the advocates of the negro have in view: they are sensible that an opinion has been generally entertained that they are identified with a political party, and influenced by very different motives from those which they publicly profess: many of the clergy of the Established Church especially have imbibed this very erroneous impression, and too frequently stand aloof from the public proceedings of Anti-Slavery advocates, lest they should be challenged with unbecoming interference in political controversy, or involve themselves with party connexions. The Committee deeply lament this error, and absolutely deny the charge: they attach themselves to no party: they solemnly disclaim all political alliance as respects this object, and therefore they protest against the injustice of arraying the opposition of political party against them: they might support their disclaimer by appealing to the avowed principles of many of their coadjutors; but they prefer calling attention to the explicit and decided language of the Letter of Instructions to their agents: *these are the only instructions* which have been given, and every person, more especially every minister of God, who has been deterred from joining the Society by such misrepresentations, is entreated candidly to peruse these instructions, and to *judge for himself whether they do not deprive his conscience of every apology* for remaining neutral or inactive in this truly Christian cause.

Finally, the Committee are persuaded that a persevering appeal at once to the understanding and to the conscience of the British public, was never yet made in vain, and they therefore would strenuously impress on the mind of every sincere friend of the cause, the importance of advocating it, not as the measure of a religious or a political party, but on the broad and acknowledged principles of civil justice and Christian duty.

5. FROM *Memoir of William Knibb, Missionary of Jamaica,* by John Howard Hinton (London, 1847)

He commenced thus:—

"Mr. Chairman, my fellow-countrymen,—I appear before you, on the present occasion, to answer those charges which have been publicly made against me by the accredited agent of the West Indian party, within the walls of this room. I wish, before I commence, to remove an impression which I suspect has been created—that I have frequently been challenged to a public discussion, and that I have refused to meet my opponent. When I was in Scotland charges were made against me and, through the press, I challenged any man, or set of men, on earth, to come forward like men, and prove the same. When I was at Cheltenham, I as publicly challenged the advocates of slavery there. But it is not to be expected that I can run up and down the land, to meet challenges of which I never hear except through the public prints. Mr. Borthwick would fain have you believe that he has been traversing the earth in search of me, and that I, appalled at the sound of his approach, have fled before him. Had he wished, really wished to meet me, why did he not cross the Tweed? He knew I was in Scotland. One of the most serious charges he brings forward is said to have occurred in Edinburgh; but he knows too well what awaits him there ever to trust himself near Dalkeith. To me there is nothing more delightful than to appear before a British audience, to clear my character from the charges that have been brought against me, and to advocate the cause of the oppressed, the injured, the despised, and persecuted African. Well am I aware of the scorn that will be cast upon my character; well am I aware of the obloquy that will attach to my name; but I fear it not; I have counted the cost; and as long as blood flows through these veins, as long as this heart beats, it shall beat for liberty and for the injured slave."

Some of the charges which Borthwick had brought against Knibb were of the gravest kind, but they were as audacious as they were grave. He had denounced him, for example, as guilty of misprision of treason. When the ground of this charge was demanded, it was laid solely in the allegation that, two or three months before the insurrection, he had said to some negroes, "Did you ever hear the *buckra* (white man) tell you anything that was good?" Ludicrously inadequate as a ground of accusation, the allegation was untrue in fact. What Knibb had said was, "Did you ever hear your *busha* (the superintendent of the floggings) tell you anything that was good?" And the circumstances was as shamefully misinterpreted as falsely cited. The words were used only for the purpose of convincing some negroes, to whom their busha had said that free papers were coming, that there was no truth in the statement.

Borthwick had said that Knibb would have been hung but for the leniency of the planters, and the inadmissibility of slave-evidence. The answer to this was that, in violation of the law, slave-evidence had been admitted against him, and that even with this advantage, the attorney-general threw up his brief in despair.

According to the statement supplied to Knibb, Mr. Borthwick had affirmed that the whole insurrection was planned in a baptist chapel, and by a baptist leader. A part of this allegation Mr. B. now wished to withdraw, asserting that he had not said that the insurrection was planned "in a baptist chapel," but somewhere "after morning prayers at a baptist chapel;" but many persons in the meeting, and on the platform Mr. (now Dr. T.) Price, held him to the words. Not a single part of the statement, however, was true.

Another statement made by Mr. Borthwick was that horrible cruelties had been perpetrated by the black baptists, especially on a young lady; a statement which, being utterly unsupported by evidence, needed no reply.

Mr. Borthwick had searched the speeches of Knibb with no very candid eye, in order to find in them materials for charging him with contradiction or impropriety; and considering the exciting circumstances under which Knibb had spoken, it would not have been surprising if his opponent had reaped some small harvest in this field. The charges thus arising, however, were but two.

The first was that, in his speech at Reading, Knibb had stated that *he had seen* more than a hundred persons hanging on one gallows, whereas he had stated in his evidence before the House of Commons that he had *not seen* many executions. His reply to this consisted in producing the printed report of his speech, and reading the passage alleged, which ran thus, "There have been (not *I have seen*) more than a hundred persons hanging on one gallows."

The second and more material charge of this class was that, at a meeting in Edinburgh, on the 19th of October, Knibb had stated that the man who planned the insurrection was a fine negro, and that he

deserved an imperishable monument. Knibb demurred to the accuracy
of this representation. "I believe I stated at Edinburgh," said he, "that,
if Sam Sharp had been a Polish nobleman, and had taken the same
measures to free the Poles from the grasp of the Russians that he took
to free his countrymen from the grasp of the slave-owner, many in
England would have said that, instead of being considered a rebel, he
deserved an imperishable monument." So much importance was
attached by Mr. Borthwick to the question whether Knibb actually
used the words alleged, that he took the trouble to procure two deposi-
tions on oath from gentlemen in Edinburgh, Mr. Thomas Duncan and
Mr. Archibald Brown, to that effect. To counteract the tendency of these
documents, Knibb subsequently obtained letters from five gentlemen,
Messrs. Ogilvey, Dickie, Alexander, Ritchie, and Wigham, affirming
their belief that the words imputed by the *Edinburgh Evening Post* were
not used. The originals of these letters are in my possession, and the
letters themselves are printed as an appendix to the report of the
proceedings at Bath. Under the circumstances, it is fair, I think, to
conclude that Knibb's version of his speech is the correct one, and to
hold him responsible for nothing beyond it. The sentiment thus
conveyed was little more than the echo of that which had repeatedly
burst from the public meetings he had addressed. "Frequently during
my tour," said he, "especially in Birmingham, in London, and in
Manchester, I have been called to order by the audience for daring,
before a British public, to call that man a rebel who only fought for his
freedom." With the facts, not merely of universal, but especially of
English history before us, it is hard to impugn this sentiment. At Bath
Knibb left the matter thus:—"It is asserted that language like this is
treason: then try me for treason, and a jury of my countrymen will award
me that justice which is my due."

After answering *seriatim* the charges I have enumerated, Knibb
concluded this part of his speech in the following terms:—

"I have now, I believe, answered every charge my opponent has
brought against me, and shown their fallacy. My character he has
attacked in the most violent manner. Did I wish to retaliate, nothing
were more easy. I have been at Dalkeith; I know the tergiversations of
Mr. B.; and if he has any regard to himself, I would warn him to let the
characters of others alone. I congratulate the West Indians on their
champion. Their cause I have no doubt will prosper in his hands. When
I think of the petty frauds they indulge to support their death-struck
cause, I cannot forbear exclaiming, Poor West Indians! Poor West
Indians! By the straitness of the siege wherewith your enemies have

besieged you, an ass's head is sold for four-score pieces of silver, and the fourth part of a cab of dove's dung for five pieces of silver.' "

He then entered at great length into the general questions of the insurrection and the abolition of slavery, winding up with the following peroration:—

"I call upon you by the tender sympathies of your nature—I call upon you by that manly feeling which Britons have ever expressed—I call upon you by the love of liberty which now animates every breast, to leave no method untried till colonial slavery shall have passed away, and became a tale of yesterday. Already the system shakes to its foundation: the passing of the Reform Bill will hasten its destruction. It needs but a united effort, (do not the elections show it?) and soon the accursed system will be cast down. Over it we will wave the banner of freedom: our chapels, again erected, shall stand monuments of that freedom; and as we retire from the spot on which we have achieved the greatest victory that ever signalized our land, we will sing, Glory to God in the highest; on earth peace, good-will towards men.' The advocates of colonial slavery know well they are not celebrating the triumph of their system, but assisting at its funeral obsequies. The sooner we arrive at the tomb the better, and then with one uplifted voice, and with one consecrated heart, we will exclaim, 'ashes to ashes, and dust to dust.' "

Mr. Borthwick's speech, which followed, was characterized by a distinct abandonment of the heaviest charges he had formerly adduced against Knibb, and by a careful avoidance of the violent language he had employed. "So far as Jamaica was concerned," he said, "he had now no quarrel with Mr. Knibb; his quarrel with him rested entirely and solely on his speeches delivered in this country."

After Mr. Borthwick had spoken, the chairman requested that those who were satisfied with Knibb's explanation would hold up their hands —then the contrary; both exhibitions being large, and received with "immense cheering" by the respective parties. The chairman declared the meeting dissolved; but, as an understanding seemed to exist that Knibb was to have an opportunity of replying to Mr. Borthwick, his friends were unwilling to disperse. After a time, consequently, another chairman, Mr. Hunt, was chosen, and Knibb again addressed such portion of the meeting as remained. Having taken up in his rejoinder the principal points of his accuser's speech, he thus concluded his address:—

"Let all the Mr. Borthwicks on earth try to continue the system of slavery by pleading for gradual emancipation, they cannot succeed. The fiat of destruction against oppression has gone forth; slavery has heard the award of her doom. Attempt to arrest the sun in his course, to stay the wheels of nature, or to dry up the ocean, ere you try to convince a free and enlightened people that slavery is the only blessing that has survived the fall, or that the happiness of a nation depends upon the oppression of man.

"Africa, thou shalt be free! Britons, patriots, fathers, females, join me in my endeavours to rid my country of this Moloch of iniquity! Let not fear, let not scorn, let not danger deter your course. Long-delayed justice demands it—mercy beseeches it—every feeling of humanity urges us forward—and every attribute of Deity is engaged on our side. If we are united, the bonds of the slave will be broken; his fetters will be snapped; the tears of the female African shall cease to flow; the trumpet of Jubilee shall sound; the banner of freedom shall be unfurled, and beneath its life-giving shade, Africa shall arise and call you blessed. Anarchy and confusion shall be banished from the earth, peace shall be restored, joy shall beam in every eye, happiness shall reign in every heart, and plenty shall open her stores to bless mankind, while the God and father of the oppressed shall smile upon the work which justice demanded, and which Britain has achieved! Remember that I plead for liberty—for liberty for those who have never forfeited it, and that without this blessing Africa must be miserable. For

> ' 'Tis liberty alone that gives the flower
> Of life its lustre and perfume,
> And we are weeds without it.' "

A show of hands being now taken, a decided majority appeared in favour of Knibb; a result, however, which is rather to be ascribed to the absence of many of the opposite party, than to any change of opinion on the part of the meeting. Both parties probably were as well convinced at first as at last. The result of this contest was, that while the West Indians substantially rewarded Borthwick, and boasted of his success, his attack on Knibb left no injurious impression on the public mind, and created no obstruction to the progress of anti-slavery agitation. His efforts may be compared to some fragment of a frowning precipice, which, falling with threatening impetuosity into the torrent that rushes below, for a moment adds to the foam, and then finds a peaceful bed beneath the uninterrupted waters.

6. FROM *Substance of An Address To The Ladies of Glasgow and Vicinity On Negro Emancipation—Mr Anderson's Chapel—5 March, 1833,* by George Thompson (Glasgow, 1833)

I have been introduced to you by your venerable Chairman as no longer a stranger, but naturalised amongst you; and am therefore encouraged to believe, that in every individual before me, I behold a kind, indulgent, and sympathising friend: brought hither,—not by the irresistible charm of novelty, but attachment to that cause, as the humble advocate of which, I have become so speedily and so widely known to you. How then can I gaze upon this vast congregation of the friends of the Negro and myself, and not be cheered, and thrilled, and animated ? Never did I feel myself more deeply affected by any spectacle than the present—never more assured that our holy undertaking must quickly and triumphantly accomplish its object;—these are signs of the times which cannot be misunderstood—"he who runs may read," that the reign of despotism is drawing to a close—the women of England and of Scotland are coming forth in the might of their majesty and mercy, and the fervour of their zeal must soon dissolve the fetters of the Slave. (Cheers.) Women of Glasgow! you have done well in coming from your homes this morning to testify your affection for the cause of liberty— you will not lose your reward—you will send through your land a kindred flame, and summon thousands of your sex to your help in the work of Emancipation. Grant me now your attention while I endeavour to strengthen your convictions of the justice of our cause, and increase your zeal in its behalf, by offering to your notice a few remarks, calculated, in my opinion, to effect these desirable ends.

There is one branch of the momentous question of Negro Emancipation, upon which I beg to fix your very serious consideration.

1. Because it has been set up as a justification of Slavery, as it now exists in our dominions.

2. Because the apology I refer to, appeals to the feelings of that portion of the community, which, above all others, I am desirous of seeing amongst the friends of Negro Emancipation.

3. Because it involves the high consideration, whether unto us belongs a discretionary power to act towards our fellow-men as we are now acting towards our Colonial bondsmen; and,

4. Because it affects the honour and equity of that Being who hath commanded us to "love our neighbour as ourselves," and to do unto others as we would that they should do unto us.

That part of the subject is this; *The abstract sinfulness of holding men in personal thraldom.* In other words, *Can any circumstances justify men in holding their fellow-men in bondage?*

In answer to this inquiry, I would unhesitatingly answer, Yes. There are circumstances during the continuance of which men may hold their fellow-creatures in slavery without incurring guilt by so doing: and the existence or non-existence of such circumstances, creates the justification, or occasions the guilt, of the man-stealer or slave-holder. When these circumstances are present, he is justified; when they are absent, he is guilty. These circumstances I will presently specify.

Is it sinful to frame unequal laws; oppressing the poor and defending the rich? If it be, then let British Colonial Slavery come to an end, for the laws it has originated are of the most unrighteous and partial description. "What is tolerable in the white man, is punished in the black; what is a venial fault in the master, is highly criminal in the slave; and criminality and punishment have a relation to the different offenders precisely the reverse of what they have in all other cases. In the laws of God, and in all human laws which are founded in justice, superior advantages render men more responsible, and, of course, give to their bad actions a higher degree of criminality: but in the Colonies the educated white is considered in the eye of the law as less guilty, and the poor ignorant black the greater delinquent. The law is fastidiously delicate in punishing the master, but ruthless and vindictive when the slave is concerned. Till of late years the slave was liable to the punishment of death for almost every thing; he might, in some colonies, be mutilated for the act of running away from severe usage; for endeavouring, by force, to break his chains, he might be burnt alive by inches, or hung up to perish in a cage." I should be compelled to detain you to an unwarrantable length if I attempted to travel through the laws of the Colonies, and point out all the perversions of law and justice which they exhibit. I will only notice the boasted slave code of Jamaica, framed in the month of February, 1831, the *ne plus ultra* of legislative wisdom for the government and *protection* of 330,000 slaves.

Let us not forget, in our consideration of the present question, our awful individual responsibility to heaven for the employment of every degree of influence in society which we possess. If we have the power of mitigating the horrors of this hateful system; if, further, we possess the ability to effect its total overthrow; then we are ourselves responsible for the continuance of the system with all its attendant horrors and enormities. We become, in a solemn and impressive sense, the possessors of these rational and immortal beings: and how shall we answer to Him who made them, if we neglect or refuse to exert ourselves in their behalf? Let us remember that they are God's creatures, created by the same power, sustained by the same goodness, bought with the same price as ourselves; that they have a capacity for suffering and enjoyment like our own, and that yet we, notwithstanding, suffer them to be bought, sold, fettered, flogged, tasked, toiled, insulted, inflamed, degraded, despised, betrayed, and butchered. We allow this in despite of reason, revelation, truth, justice, humanity, and love. O think of these things, and weep for your country and for yourselves! Think of these things, and let your zeal be enkindled and your pity excited, that your exertions may henceforth be commensurate with the miseries of these unhappy beings, and your own responsibility. Remember what they might have been, and what they *are*. They might have been virtuous; but they are deeply sunk in vice. They might have been enlightened; but they are enshrouded in thick darkness. They might, perchance, have been Christians; but they are miserable heathens. They might have been soaring to heaven; but they are eating and toiling with the beast. They might have been fulfilling the true purposes of life; but they are debased to the condition of crawling slaves, who must be driven to their beastlike occupations by the most horrible scourge in the world. Remember that all this vice, and darkness, and heathenism, and prostration of soul, and degradation of body, and perversion of mind, are chargeable upon *us*, who have permitted them to be impiously seized, and held in thraldom to the present hour.

See the demoralizing effects of the system, manifested in the conduct of its abettors at home. Direct your attention for a moment to a great meeting of West Indians, for the purpose of promoting what they call the welfare of the colonies. Such a meeting was held some time ago in London. British Peers, and Commoners, and Merchants, and Aldermen, and other high professional and mercantile gentlemen, were assembled, —many of them solemnly sworn to defend the liberties and rights of every unoffending subject of the realm. What did they do? Did they show any pity for the slave? No.—Did they exhibit any regard for the eternal principles of truth, justice, and equity? No.—Any attachment to the cause of religion? No. They fiercely denounced, what?—wrong? no;—cruelty? no;—oppression? no:—But the measures of the government then recently brought forward for the amelioration of the condition of the slave. They styled such interference unjust, monstrous, unheard of, and iniquitous. They displayed an unbending attachment—to what?—mercy? no;—humanity? no;—*to money*! Each seemed to say,

"Mammon, thou art my god, and I will worship thee." Did they denounce the Courant? No.—Did they condemn the treatment the Missionaries had just experienced? No.—Did they propose a measure of emancipation of any kind? They did not. There was a scrupulous avoidance of all the real facts and merits of the case. Many things were said about the worth of the Colonies; the export and import dues; the amount of tonnage in the shipping; the number of seamen employed; the past greatness and present distresses of the Colonies; the necessity of instant relief for the Planter;—but not one word about the compromise of national honour; or the forfeiture of national independence; or the wants and claims, and natural and inalienable rights of the Slave; or the sacred duties and obligations of religion. Nothing could exceed their acute sensibility on the subject of their own wrongs; *their* honour, and character, and comfort, and wealth, and independence, were all matters of the highest possible importance, and were ably and eloquently expatiated upon. But not one word was said in vindication of the natural rights of 700,000 unoffending human beings, although their happiness and welfare were bound up in the question they were met to discuss. O how disgusting to see men of rank, and wealth, and influence, and high profession, thus selfishly struggling for money,—for polluted blood-stained money; and consenting to obtain it at the expense of the happiness and liberties of their fellow-men!

See the nature of Slavery further illustrated in the recent transactions and present aspect of Jamaica. The massacre of slaves; the persecution of Missionaries; the destruction of chapels; the rejection of religion. A band of civilized barbarians in the shape of white magistrates, officers of militia, planters, merchants, &c. cheered on by a preacher of the Gospels, to deeds of spoliation and blood; and forming unions for the banishment of the shepherd and the destruction of the flock. A House of Assembly upholding cruelty, fostering despotism, desecrating religion, reviling the constitution, resisting the government, and threatening the overthrow of a part of the British empire. A degraded, enslaved, terrified, black population on the one side; an infuriated, blood-thirsty, and infatuated confederacy of white slave-mongers on the other. A race of men dying under the hand of oppression: if quiet, toiling and expiring in unmitigated captivity; if murmuring or resisting, visited with the whip, the dungeon, the rack, the gibbet, the bayonet, or the musket-ball.

If for these things the judgment of God should come upon us, we cannot say we have not been warned. Rolling thunders, and sweeping hurricanes, and wild tornadoes, and desolating earthquakes, and raging fevers, and declining commerce, and a dying population, and weeping mercy, and insulted justice, and reason, and religion, and God, have said again and again, "Let these people go." Their voices are still heard; let us, though late, obey. Women of Scotland! hear you not their voices to-day? will you not make this question peculiarly your own?

There are many of the evils of Slavery which you can more fully appreciate than ourselves. You can enter into the feelings of mothers torn from their children; and wives severed from their husbands for ever.

> " E'en this last wretched boon their foes deny,
>   To live together, or together die;
>   By felon hands, by one relentless stroke,
>   See the fond link of feeling nature broke;
>   The fibres twisting round a parent's heart,
>   Torn from their grasp, and bleeding as they part."

You can estimate the situation of those wretched mothers who are doomed to commit the nurture of their children to others; whose daughters are liable to the assaults of wicked and evil-disposed men; who are prevented frequently from marrying, by the dislike which the negroes have to see their wives indecently exposed and cruelly flogged at the command of a merciless master. I may be accused of appealing to your feelings while I state facts like these. But is not the question we are discussing a question of feeling? Does not the negro mother feel when she consigns her offspring to the care of another? Does she not feel when she looks upon her child, and reads "slave" written upon its joyous brow, and remembers that those limbs may be some day loaded with manacles; that body lacerated with the whip; that brow overcast with sullenness and despair; that frame exhausted by unrewarded toil; and that life shortened by accumulated privations and sufferings!

This is a question interesting to you who are of the softer sex, because to you is committed the training of our infant population. It is yours

> " To pour the fresh instruction o'er the mind,
>   To breathe the enlivening spirit, and to fix
>   The generous purpose in the glowing breast."

Will you not infuse into that "glowing breast" the love of liberty? Will you not teach your infants to pity and relieve the captive? Will you not inspire them with a hatred of despotism? Will you not teach them in their youth to say, "the liberty we love we will bestow"? Women of Scotland! be encouraged. The wise, and the noble, and the good, are with you in this great cause. Colonial despotism already totters,—the hand-writing is already seen upon the wall. Soon will the knell of slavery be rung, and the shout of exultation go up, "England is just,—her slaves are free."

Finally. I recommend this cause,—this good, this noble, this ennobling cause,—with its many deep and spirit-stirring interests, to your warmest zeal, your tenderest sympathies, your unceasing care, and Christian consideration. Be not surprised, still less discouraged, at the attempts made to retard its progress. It has been assailed,—it will be assailed. It has ever had its enemies,—it will ever have its enemies: but it has advanced, and will advance, to a speedy, a happy, and a glorious consummation. It rests upon the basis of Eternal Justice. It has been upreared by the hands of humanity, and benevolence, and Christian piety, and it shall still increase,—and still extend,—and still rise higher in the estimation of the great and the good, and in the approbation and patronage of heaven; and its friends, from its lofty summit, may smile defiance on its foes, while every shaft which envy, or faction, or ignorance, or malice hurls, to wound or to destroy it, lies pointless and perishing at its base. Yes! it shall stand unhurt, unsullied, and immoveable,

> " Like some tall cliff that rears its awful form,
>   Swells from the vale, and midway meets the storm;
>   Though round its breast the gathering clouds are spread,
>   Eternal sunshine settles on its head."

7. *Petitions For The Abolition of Slavery* (House of Lords, *Journals* vol. 65, 1833)

pp. 294–5 (13 May 1833)

... Petition of the members of a Society and Congregation of Wesleyan Methodists worshipping at their chapel in South Kirkly, in the County of York, whose names are thereunto subscribed; severally praying their Lordships "to concur with His Majesty's ministers in removing the great reproach and sin of slavery from our nation, by immediately recognizing the Negro as a man and granting to him all the rights of a British Subject"; and further praying their Lordships "that especial regard may be had to religious liberty in the settlement of this momentous question; and that especial care be taken to secure for the Negroes and their teachers, and all other persons in the colonies, the same Liberty of Conscience, and the same Facilities for Public Worship, as are afforded to all His Majesty's subjects in this country".

p. 299 (13 May 1833)

... Petition of the Females belonging to the Congregation of Protestant Dissenters assembling for Divine Worship in Carr's Lane Chapel, Birmingham, whose names are thereunto subscribed praying their Lordships "not to allow the pleas of interested cupidity to set aside the claims of justice and mercy, nor any partial and palliating measures of mistaken policy to be a substitute for the only safe and effectual remedy, but to abolish, immediately and entirely, slavery in the British Colonies, a system repugnant equally to the dictates of reason, humanity and religion".

8. FROM the Speech of Edward Stanley, Secretary of State For The Colonies, Introducing the Government Plan For The Emancipation of the Slaves, 14 May 1833 (Hansard, *Parliamentary Debates*, 3rd series, vol. 18, pp. 1193–1231)

This question of unparalleled importance—involving a greater amount of property—affecting the happiness and the well-being of a larger portion of individuals than was ever before brought together is rendered peculiarly difficult by the time, and from the circumstances under which it is introduced. Sir, I feel most anxious on account of the responsibility which devolves upon me. I feel not only, that our maritime commerce is here concerned—that 250,000 tons of British shipping are affected—not only that a revenue of 5,000,000l. is to be dealt with and legislated for; but I feel, that if possible, higher interests are involved—that the interests, the comforts, the prosperity, perhaps I might say the very existence, of a large population in the West-India colonies depending upon us for support and protection, hang upon the decision of those Resolutions which it will be my duty to submit to the House, . . . (1193, 1194)

Nay, Sir, I cannot submit the question even to this—I cannot deny to myself, that the happiness of the descendants of those for whom I now propose to legislate—that generations yet unborn are to be affected for good or for evil by the course which this House may think proper to adopt. Nor can I conceal from myself, or from this House, the immense influence on the population of foreign countries which must arise from the result of the mighty experiment which we now propose to make. On that may depend the welfare of millions of men in a state of slavery in colonies not belonging to Great Britain. Besides all these things, there is enough to make any man—the strongest, the boldest, and the best—shrink in some degree under the weight of so great a responsibility; for the question is now in such a state, that deal with it as you will, you can only have a choice of difficulties. Those difficulties, I assert, are all but insurmountable. They leave us only the choice of doing some good at the least risk of effecting evil. We are called upon to legislate between two conflicting parties—one deeply involved by pecuniary interests—involved, moreover, in difficulties of the most pressing character—difficulties which are now present, and are constantly increasing; the other deeply involved by their feelings and their opinions, representing a growing determination on the part of the people of this country to put an end to slavery, which no one can deny or wisely despise—a determination the more absolute, and the less resistible, because founded in sincere determination is expressed in a voice so potential, that no Minister can venture to disregard it. The time is, indeed, gone by when the question can be for a moment entertained whether or not this system can be made perpetual; the only point we can discuss—the only point we shall discuss is the safest, speediest, happiest way in which to effect its final and entire abolition. And let me say, that they who characterize this as a mere ebullition of popular feeling—as transient in its character—as fleeting or unsubstantial—the mere expression of yesterday—are but deceiving themselves; for it is not of late or of momentary birth, but springs from the deep-settled and long-entertained convictions of reflecting men—from that same spirit of lasting humanity, which, fifty years ago, pressed on the Parliament of that day; and which, in defiance of the arguments, that we should ruin our trade—in defiance of opposition from many quarters—compelled the Parliament to abolish for ever that iniquitous and disgraceful trade by which supplies of human flesh were obtained from the shores of Africa. If there are, Sir, any persons who can doubt that the authors of that politic and humane and just abolition looked forward to the emancipation of the slaves as the consequence of abolishing the Slave Trade, I would beg leave to refer them to the speeches of the most distinguished advocates of that humane measure. Sir, when we look back to the language of the great men who introduced that measure into Parliament, and who so zealously laboured for the accomplishment of that object, which they at length almost achieved, leaving little for those to do who actually accomplished it, we find that, although the two questions were carefully separated at the time, the gradual abolition of slavery remained upon their minds, and was distinguishable in the expression of their feelings in the debates of that day, as necessarily and inseparably connected with that preliminary step of the abolition of the slave-trade. (1195) . . .

I trouble the House with these extracts to prove that the feeling which now pervades the country is not of this day's growth; but that the people of this country have long considered it expedient—have long held it a duty, on the ground of religion and of justice, to advance any measure which might tend to the early abolition of this disgraceful system. The nation have now loudly, and for a length of time declared that the disgrace of slavery should not be suffered to remain part of our national system. (1197) . . .

I will not deny, that if we look to the measures agreed upon by the Colonial Legislatures since the period I have alluded to, some improvements may be found in points affecting the physical condition of the slaves; but I do assert boldly, and without fear of contradiction even from themselves, that nothing has been done of that nature, extent, or character, which may fairly be characterized as a step towards the ultimate extermination of the system. (1198) . . .

I am now addressing Parliament in 1833; and up to this hour the voice neither of friendly expostulation nor of authority has produced the desired effect upon the Colonial Legislatures—not a single step had been taken by any of them with a view to the extinction of negro slavery. Undoubtedly some of the colonies have been engaged on plans— or rather shadows and outlines of plans; but none of them have been founded in truth or justice, least of all on those recommendations forwarded from the Government at home. But with regard to any real effort—to any substantial and positive improvement—to the institution of an officer as protector of the slaves—an officer appointed by the Crown—really and truly their guardian and counsel—one independent of the planters—of all local influence, and all local friendship—in no one colony has such a thing been attempted—in no one colony, Sir, has this efficient protector been appointed. Undoubtedly there have been Councils of Protection—any two Magistrates might act as a Council of Protection. Means have been afforded of facilitating the acquisition of legal rights; but to whom have the trusts in such cases been delegated? To those who have an interest in suppressing slavery? No, but to those who are themselves the possessors of slaves, and who have an unequivocal interest in the existence of slavery, and who are involved in the feelings and prejudices of the Colonial Legislatures. It may be said, that this is compliance. So it is—but it is a species of compliance worse than a mockery. It gives the shadow, but lets slip the substance; and it is only done to afford a pretext for saying "You have no right to interfere; we have not exactly appointed protectors of slaves, but we have put the slaves under protection in reality as effectual and as advantageous." (1202) . . .

But what will the Committee think of the readiness of the Colonial Legislatures (I speak, God knows, not in bitterness but in sorrow), when I say, that up to this hour no one colony has abolished the practice of inflicting corporal punishment upon females. They have, indeed, in some degree, restrained it; but by restraining they recognize the principle: they have guarded against indecency, but they have not yet carried into effect that which in all the nations of the world has been the first step towards civilization—the raising the female sex from a state of degradation to that of equality and a sense of delicacy. Talk of preparing the slave for freedom! of ripening his moral faculties, to render him capable of enjoying it, and yet show him that all his dearest and domestic ties may be violated—that his wife, his daughter, or his sister, may be subjected to. . . . (1202). . .

But how can you tell the negro that he shall look up as a free man—but can you talk of hopes, encouragement—preparation for individual freedom, and general emancipation, when even at this moment the slave dares not raise his eyes to his master's face without the risk of receiving thirty-nine lashes ? I do not speak of the actual exercise of any such power—I do not believe it could be exercised—but that such a power exists there can be no doubt. In case of unjust infliction, the slave must go before two Magistrates, themselves slave-masters; and if he can persuade them to believe him, the master is to be prosecuted, and if found guilty by a Jury, subjected to fine and imprisonment; but if the Magistrates think the evidence is insufficient, without any malicious motive on the part of the slave, he is to be subjected to a second flogging for having made the complaint. This is the practical working in Jamaica of the law in favour of the slave. But there is a further punishment:—in case aggravated, overwhelming cruelty, be proved against a master, if a Jury find that it has been atrocious, then an addition is to made to the fine and imprisonment; and what is it ? That the slave may be sold, and the money handed over to the criminal master. This is the punishment inflicted on masters in Jamaica for conduct which is called atrocious. (1203) . . .

I allude to the institution of marriage. Objections have been removed: but as I can see there has been no discouragement of a different course either on the part of the Legislature or the planters, no means have been taken to impress on the minds of the slaves the sanctity of the slaves, sanctity of the ceremony, or the sacredness of the obligation. A little has been done to remove formal and local obstacles, and to allow marriages to be contracted; but they are subject to the will of the owner, and in some cases a certificate of a clergyman of the Church of England, or of a Dissenting Minister, is also necessary. I will now advert to the point of slave evidence. Perhaps, in going through these points, the House thinks I am entering more at length into the subject than is requisite; but when I am recommending to Parliament to take a step of so much importance, I feel it my duty to show, that all these local enactments have more of shadow than substance, and that there has been little or no disposition to fill up the outline chalked out by the mother country. (1203, 1204).

I hold in my hand a passage, from a speech delivered by Mr. Canning in 1799, which, long as it is, I shall take the liberty of reading, because it shows how naturally and how strongly the ardent feelings of his mind were then directed to this subject, which afterwards occupied his most anxious thoughts when he became the great ornament to the Senate. I feel fully persuaded that the House will not think I am wasting its time. It was delivered in reply to Sir William Young, in a debate on the subject of the slave trade; and I entreat the House. in following me, to substitute for slave trade the system of slavery, and every syllable will be applicable to the present condition of the question:—The question is, whether, in what is to be done towards alleviating and finally extinguishing the horrors of the slave trade, the proper agent was the British House of Commons, or the Colonial Assemblies? The hon. Baronet contended that the Colonial Assemblies, and not the British House of Commons, were the agents most proper to be employed. But what was the hon. Baronet's argument? "Trust not the masters of slaves in what concerns legislation for slavery! However specious their laws may appear, depend upon it they must be ineffectual in their application. It is in the nature of things that they should be so." Granted. Let then the British House of Commons do their part themselves! Let them not delegate the trust of doing it to those who, according to the hon. Baronet's testimony, cannot execute that trust fairly. Let the evils of the slave trade presents as utterly unqualified for the undertaking—not by the masters of slaves! Their laws, the hon. Baronet had avowed, could never reach, would never cure, the evil. . . . There was something in the nature of absolute authority in the relation between master and slave, which made despotism, in all cases, and under all circumstances, an incompetent and unsure executor even of its own provisions in favour of the objects of its power. As I before remarked, let any Gentleman substitute "Abolition of Slavery" for "Abolition of the Slave Trade;" and there is not an argument advanced by Mr. Canning, in 1799, that may not be used with double force now, to justify the interference of Parliament. (1206) . . .

Now, that is surely a state of things not arising from any proceedings in this House, or in this country, and there is nothing can be done to relieve the West-India interest in a commercial or trading point of view, otherwise than by reducing the amount of sugar produced, or by calling into existence fresh markets for its consumption, so that the demand shall come fully up to the supply. New land has been brought into cultivation; new colonies have been added to our possessions; the cultivators of the old land have been compelled to adopt new and improved modes of increasing the productive powers of their estates, and all for the purpose of contributing to swell that vast amount of excessive production which, beyond all dispute, is the great source of the present difficulties of the West-India interest. The owners of property in the West-Indies proceed with enterprises not warranted by the circumstances of the colonies, or the demand for sugar in the European markets; they find themselves involved in difficulties, and they seek to escape from those difficulties by means which only involve them in fresh entanglements; and then they turn round and impute all the blame to what they call the fanatical proceedings which it is said had their origin in this House in the year 1823. (1210) ...

I will suppose, that the agitation so often referred to has been the cause of the present state of things in the colonies; and now I ask, what can we do to remove that cause—what is the remedy? It is very easy to say we will exclude, or we might have excluded, all knowledge of those proceedings from the colonies. I say you could have done no such thing, and still less can you do it for the future. . . . You cannot prevent the voice of the people from being heard within these walls and you cannot prevent the sound of what passes here from reaching the colonies —it will not only reach the colonies, but it will reach the slaves themselves, aggravated by the incautious comments of those who may become the medium of communicating it to the negro population of the West-Indies. I repeat it, that if you wish to stop the progress of this species of information, it is out of your power. The only course left to you is to advance. The only dangerous course is happily impracticable—you cannot recede—you cannot stand still. It has been said, that "the best mode of avoiding danger is to face it". I say that in this case the only possible mode of coping with the danger, so as to afford the smallest chance of safety, is by manfully grappling with it in front. Various objections have been raised to measures founded upon propositions for ameliorating the condition of the slaves, and the strongest apprehensions have been expressed lest we should proceed with steps too hasty and upon data not carefully examined; it is said, that you must render the slave fit for freedom before you offer him emancipation, otherwise you entail nothing but misery upon the negro, and ruin upon the planter. We are told, too, that the effect of such a proceeding will necessarily be to cause a great diminution in the amount of production, that it will be absolutely impracticable to cultivate sugar, that the colonies must be thrown up, and that nothing but ruin will. . . . Sir so far as the amount of the diminution of that production would be matter of regret—I am not quite certain, that it might not be for the benefit of the planters and of the colonies themselves, in the end, if that production were in some degree diminished. But the question for the consideration of the House is, will you, with the statement which I shall have the honour of laying before you—will you, looking to that statement supported by facts and figures alone—will you encourage and defend the system by which the present extent and amount of production are maintained? (1211, 1212) . . .

Thus invariably, with two single exceptions [Jamaica and Demerara], in these colonies we find, while the slave population is fast decreasing, the production of sugar is increasing to a very considerable extent. (1213) . . .

I will not impute any guilt to the owners of the slaves—I will not impute to them anything more than that perversion of moral feeling which it is one of the greatest curses of slavery, that it entails and impresses upon the mind of the enslaver—I will not impute any want of the ordinary feelings of humanity, further than that they are perverted by prejudice, and rendered callous by custom and habit—but I call upon the House to consider where punishments are unrecorded, where no check is interposed by the legal authority, where no remedy, or no efficient remedy is given to the slave by authority of the law—to consider if, in this comparatively free state of Demerara, this be the amount of punishment inflicted in one year; what must be the nature of the system which is carried on in other colonies, where there are no checks?—what must be the degradation of the system under which the other colonies of the British Empire at this moment labour? What is the amount of unredressed injustice—what is to regulate, by interposing its solemn authority between this dreadful system of oppression, and that which Mr. Canning called 'the abstract love of the cartwhip!'' I am aware that we have been often taunted with our ignorance of the negro character; my belief is, that any man may inform himself sufficiently on that point, and that we commit a grievous error when we suppose that the moral circumstances attendant upon slavery have so changed the physical character of the negro as to unfit him for freedom. It is a most dangerous error to attribute that to the physical qualities of the negro which results solely from the moral conditions which slavery has superinduced. (1215, 1216).

The whole of this argument amounts to saying, that the negroes are not fit for emancipation, and that we must wait until they are; and that argument, if it be good for anything, goes too far; for it proceeds to the indefinite conclusion, that we must postpone emancipation, not for ten or twenty or thirty years, but to some period no one can say how remote. I know that people will tell me we do not wish to perpetuate slavery—we merely wish to postpone it till the negroes are fit for freedom—till they manifest a disposition for laborious industry sufficient to qualify them for the privileges of free men. That argument, if it proves anything, proves too much, will that ever take place, so long as depopulating influence of slavery prevails? We are told that the negroes own no domestic ties; nor will they, so long as you keep them in that state of slavery which debases their principles, and which deprives them of foresight, and which takes away from them the motives to industry. The slaves have no education, and you deny them any; for, as slaves, they can have none. They have hitherto been treated as chattels attached to the soil—do you think they can be made fit for freedom, till freedom has exercised its influence upon their minds and upon their moral character? *The treatment* of the West-India *negroes is a stain upon* a Christian age, and *upon* a country professing *itself* Christian. If the slaves be made acquainted with religion, they must learn that slavery is inconsistent with the Christian religion; and will you shut out religion, in order that you may maintain slavery? Other countries have read us a severe lesson upon this subject. In colonies belonging to Catholic countries, no man was allowed to possess a slave, who did not provide the means of instructing him in the Catholic faith. Be that, however, as it may, this I will say, that this House will ill discharge its duty, if it does not forthwith put forth a declaration of religious freedom, as respects the colonies, and does not compel the local authorities to leave to every negro within their limits, the free, independent, and inviolable right of adopting whatever form of Christianity he may think proper. (1216, 1217) ...

I do not credit what some people say about the negro character; but I do credit what is said about the slave character. I know the effect of a tropical climate. The effect of the state of slavery in these countries is to inculcate upon the slave, that labour is the greatest of all curses, and that the removal of labour is the greatest of all blessings. To throw the slave suddenly into freedom would be to destroy all his inclinations to industry; it would be exposing him to the temptation of recurring to his primitive habits of savage life, from which he has but lately been reclaimed. Therefore some restriction is necessary for a time, both for the masters, and for the good of the slaves themselves. I know no better security which can be devised, than that which I propose, by obliging the masters to fix a value upon their slaves, and afterwards regulating the rate of wages can be fixed. (1224, 1225). ...

When brought into the market, West-India property undoubtedly has sustained a fearful depreciation; but, in order to ascertain the real state of the case, let us look at the rate of profits; and in doing so we have a sure guide in the statements put forth by the West-India proprietors themselves; I allude to the returns presented by them to the Board of Trade, and these returns have the evidence of the West-India proprietors as to the cost of raising every hogshead of sugar, and also as to the number of hogsheads imported annually, and the net profit upon each. It appears that the net profit arising from the cultivation of sugar is 1,200,000l. a-year. We have not equally accurate data for calculating the net profits upon rum and coffee; but, assuming it, and I am not far wrong in doing so, to be between 250,000l. and 300,000l. a-year, the total net profit of West-India property will amount to 1,500,000l. annually. We propose to advance a loan to the planters, amounting to ten years purchase of those profits. We propose a loan to the West-India Planters of 15,000,000l. It will be a question for Parliament to decide in what manner and on what conditions that loan shall be granted, and how it shall be repaid. (1226) . . .

We are about to emancipate the slaves; the old, after a trial of their industrious and other good qualities—the young immediately. With the young, therefore, our responsibility will immediately commence. If we place them in a state of freedom, we are bound to see that they are fitted for the enjoyment of that state; we are bound to give them the means of proving to themselves that the world is not for merely animal existence—that it is not the lot of man merely to labour incessantly from the cradle to the grave—and that to die is not merely to get to the end of a wearisome pilgrimage. We must endeavour to give them habits, and to imbue them with feelings calculated to qualify them for the adequate discharge of their duties here; and we must endeavour to instil into them the conviction, that when those duties shall be discharged, they are not "as the brutes that perish". (1228) . . .

But I entertain a confident hope that the Resolutions which I shall have the honour to submit to the House contain a germ, which in the process of time, will be matured, by better judgment and knowledge, into a perfect fruit; and that, from the day on which the Act passes there will be secured to the country, to the colonies, and to all classes of his Majesty's subjects, the benefits of a virtual extinction of all the horrors attendant on a state of slavery; and that, at no very distant period, by no uncertain operation, but by the effect of that machinery which the proposed plan will put in motion, the dark stain which disfigures the fair freedom of this country will be wholly wiped out. Sir, in looking to this most desirable object, it is impossible not to advert to those who first broached the mighty question of the extinction of slavery, the earliest labourers in that cause, the final triumph of which they were not destined to see. They struggled for the establishment of first principles—they were satisfied with laying the foundation of that edifice which they left it to their successors to rear; they saw the future, as the prophets of old saw "the days that were to come"; but they saw it afar off, and with the eye of faith. It is not without the deepest emotion I recollect that there is yet living one of the earliest, one of the most religious, one of the most conscientious, one of the most eloquent, one of the most zealous friends of this great cause, who watched it in its dawn. Wilberforce still remains to see, I trust, the final consummation of the great and glorious work which he was one of the first to commence; and to exclaim, like the last of the prophets to whom I have already alluded: "Lord, now let thy servant depart in peace." Sir, it is with great regret that I have felt it necessary to detain the House so long; but on a subject of so much difficulty, it was imperative upon me to do so. I will now, however, after thanking the House for the patience and attention with which they have been so good as to listen to me, conclude with offering up an ardent prayer, that by the course which they may adopt, they will for a second time set the world a glorious example of a commercial nation, weighing commercial advantages light in extinguishing slavery, gradually, safely, but at the same time completely; a result the more to be desired, if accomplished by a yielding on one side and the other, which may make both sides forget extreme opinion; and which will exhibit a great and proud example of a deliberative assembly, reconciling conflicting interests, liberating the slave without inflicting hardship on his master, gratifying the liberal and humane spirit of the age without harming even those who stand in its way, and vindicating their high functions by moderately, but with determination, and in a manner honourable to the people of whom they are the representatives, acting in a manner on this important question, which will afford a sure pledge of a successful termination of the glorious career on which they are about to enter. (1229, 1230)

Sir, I now beg leave to move the following Resolutions:

1. That it is the opinion of this Committee, that immediate and effectual measures be taken for the entire abolition of slavery throughout the colonies, under such provisions for regulating the condition of the Negroes, as may combine their welfare with the interests of the proprietors.

2. That it is expedient that all children born after the passing of any Act, or who shall be under the age of six years at the time of passing any Act of Parliament for this purpose, be declared free; subject, nevertheless, to such temporary restrictions as may be deemed necessary for their support and maintenance.

3. That all persons now slaves, be entitled to be registered as

apprenticed labourers, and to acquire thereby all rights and privileges of freedom; subject to the restriction of labouring, under conditions, and for a time to be fixed by Parliament, for their present owners.

4. That to provide against the risk of loss which proprietors in his Majesty's colonial possessions might sustain by the abolition of slavery, his Majesty be enabled to advance, by way of loan, to be raised from time to time, a sum not exceeding in the whole £15,000,000, to be repaid in such manner, and at such rate of interest as shall be prescribed by Parliament. (1230)

9. FROM Petition of Lords Wellington, St Vincent, Penshurst, and Wynford against the Emancipation Act, 20 August, 1833 (House of Lords, *Journals*, vol. 65, pp. 604–5)

Dissentient

1st: Because it is attempted by this Bill to emancipate a Nation of Slaves; not prepared by a previous course of Education of Religious Instruction, or of training of habits and Industry or of social Intercourse, for the position in which they will be placed in Society.

2d: Because the Value, as Possessions of the Crown of Great Britain, of the Colonies in which those Negroes are located, as well as the Value of their Estates the Proprietors and Colonists, depends upon the Labour of the Negroes, to obtain the valuable Produce of the soil, Sugar, whether as slaves as Apprentices, or as Free Labourers for hire.

3d: Because the Experience of all Times and of all Nations, particularly that of Modern Times, and in our own Colonies and in Saint Domingo, has proved that Men uncivilized, and at liberty to labour or not as they pleased, will not work for Hire at regular agricultural Labour in the Low Grounds within the Tropics; and the Example of the United States, a Country but thinly peopled in proportion to its Extent, and Fertility, and always in want of Hands, has shewn that even in more temperate Climates the Labour of emancipated Negroes themselves, required that they should be removed elsewhere.

4th: Because the Number of Negroes in the several Islands and Settlements on the Continent of America in which they are located is so small in proportion to the Extent of the Country which they occupy, and the Fertility of the Soil is so great, and the Climate, however insalubrious and little inviting to Exertion and labour is so favourable to vegetation and the Growth of all Descriptions of Produce of the Earth that it cannot be expected that these emancipated Slaves, thus uneducated and untrained, will be induced to work for hire.

5th: Because upon Speculation depends the Value of a Capital of not less than Two Hundred Millions Sterling; including therein the Fortunes and Existence in a State of Independence of Thousands of Colonists and Proprietors of Estates in the Colonies, the Trade of the Country, the Employment of 250,000 Tons of British Shipping and of 250,000 Seamen, and a Revenue which produces to the Exchequer upon Sugar alone not less than Five Millions Sterling per annum.

6th: Because the Bill, in enforcing upon the Colonists the Emancipation of their Slaves attains its object by Enactments and Measures least calculated to conciliate their Feelings and Interests, and those of the local Legislatures, by whom government in the Colonies must continue to be exercised.

7th: Because of the Details of the Measure, an Engagement made by the Proprietors of Estates in the Colonies has been violated; and a Resolution agreed to by both Houses of Parliament, and communicated to the Colonies, has been departed from, and the Period of Apprenticeship altered from twelve years to six. . . . The Colonial Legislatures must first pass certain Laws; and then Commissioners appointed under Authority of the Bill are to proceed to make a Distribution among Nineteen Colonies of the whole sum held out, according to a principle which is considered by many of the Colonial Proprietors to be partial and unjust.

8th: Because of the Extension of the Act of the 52d George 3d cap. 155, by the 61st Clause of the Bill [see Document X] to the Colonies, is not necessary for the Apprenticeship and Emancipation of the Slaves in the Colonies. It is not justified by anything that has passed, and will be considered by the Colonial Legislatures as a gratuitous Injury, and a Breach of their independent authority, as provided by the Acts of 1773 and respected from that Time to this.

10. FROM Abolition of Slavery Act 1833: 3 & 4
William IV c. 73 (*Statutes of the United
Kingdom of Great Britain and Ireland*, with
notes by N. Simons, vol. 13, London 1835)

CAP. LXXIII.

An Act for the Abolition of Slavery throughout the *British*
Colonies; for promoting the Industry of the manumitted
Slaves; and for compensating the Persons hitherto
entitled to the Services of such Slaves.

[28th *August* 1833.]

' WHEREAS divers Persons are holden in Slavery within
' divers of His Majesty's Colonies, and it is just and
' expedient that all such Persons should be manumitted
' and set free, and that a reasonable Compensation should
' be made to the Persons hitherto entitled to the Services
' of such Slaves for the Loss which they will incur by being
' deprived of their Right to such Services: and whereas it
' is also expedient that Provision should be made for
' promoting the Industry and securing the good Conduct of
' the Persons so to be manumitted, for a limitted Period
' after such their Manumission: And whereas it is
' necessary that the Laws now in force in the said several
' Colonies should forthwith be adapted to the new State
' and Relations of Society therein which will follow upon
' such general Manumission as aforesaid of the said
' Slaves; and that, in order to afford the necessary Time
' for such Adaptation of the said Laws, a short Interval
' should elapse before such Manumission should take
' effect;' be it therefore enacted by the King's most
Excellent Majesty, by and with the Advice and Consent
of the Lords Spiritual and Temporal, and Commons,
in this present Parliament assembled, and by the
Authority of the same, That from and after the First
Day of *August* One thousand eight hundred and thirty-
four all Persons who in conformity with the Laws now in
force in the said Colonies respectively shall on or before

All Persons
who on the 1st
August 1834
shall have been
registered as
Slaves, and
be Six Years

the First Day of *August* One thousand eight hundred and thirty-four have been duly registered as Slaves in any such Colony, and who on the said First Day of *August* One thousand eight hundred and thirty-four shall be actually within any such Colony, and who shall by such Registries appear to be on the said First Day of *August* One thousand eight hundred and thirty-four of the full Age of Six Years or upwards, shall by force and virtue of this Act, and without the previous Execution of any Indenture of Apprenticeship, or other Deed or Instrument for that Purpose, become and be apprenticed Labourers; provided that, for the Purposes aforesaid, every Slave engaged in his ordinary Occupation on the Seas shall be deemed and taken to be within the Colony to which such Slave shall belong. *old or upwards shall become apprenticed Labourers.*

II. And be it further enacted, That during the Continuance of the Apprenticeship of any such apprenticed Labourer such Person or Persons shall be entitled to the Services of such apprenticed Labourer as would for the Time being have been entitled to his or her Services as a Slave if this Act had not been made. *Who entitled to Services of the Slave as an apprenticed Labourer.*

III. Provided also, and be it further enacted, That all Slaves who may at any Time previous to the passing of this Act have been brought with the Consent of their Possessors, and all apprenticed Labourers who may hereafter with the like Consent be brought, into any Part of the United Kingdom of *Great Britain* and *Ireland*, shall from and after the passing of this Act be absolutely and entirely free, to all Intents and Purposes whatsoever. *Slaves brought into the United Kingdom with Consent of Possessors, free.*

IV. 'And whereas it is expedient that all such appren-
'ticed Labourers should, for the Purposes hereinafter
'mentioned, be divided into Three distinct Classes, the
'First of such Classes consisting of prædial apprenticed
'Labourers attached to the Soil, and comprising all
'Persons who in their State of Slavery were usually
'employed in Agriculture, or in the Manufacture of
'Colonial Produce or otherwise, upon Lands belonging
'to their Owners; the Second of such Classes consisting
'of prædial apprenticed Labourers not attached to the
'Soil, and comprising all Persons who in their State of
'Slavery were usually employed in Agriculture, or in the
'Manufacture of Colonial Produce or otherwise, upon *Apprenticed Labourers to be divided into Three Classes, viz. prædial attached, prædial unattached, and non-prædial.*

' Lands not belonging to their Owners; and the Third of
' such Classes consisting of non-prædial apprenticed
' Labourers, and comprising all apprenticed Labourers
' not included within either of the Two preceding Classes;'
be it therefore enacted, That such Division as aforesaid
of the said apprenticed Labourers into such Classes as
aforesaid shall be carried into effect in such Manner and
Form and subject to such Rules and Regulations as shall,
for that Purpose be established under such Authority
and in and by such Acts of Assembly, Ordinances, or
Orders in Council, as herein-after mentioned: Provided
always, that no Person of the Age of Twelve Years and
upwards shall by or by virtue of any such Act of Assembly,
Ordinance, or Order in Council, be included in either of
the said Two Classes of prædial apprenticed Labourers
unless such Person shall for Twelve Calendar Months at
the least next before the passing of this present Act have
been habitually employed in Agriculture or in the Manufacture of Colonial Produce.

Proviso.

V. And be it further enacted, That no Person who by
virtue of this Act, or of any such Act of Assembly,
Ordinance, or Order in Council as aforesaid, shall become
a prædial apprenticed Labourer, whether attached or not
attached to the Soil, shall continue in such Apprenticeship
beyond the First Day of *August* One thousand eight
hundred and forty; and that during such his or her
Apprenticeship no such prædial apprenticed Labourer,
whether attached or not attached to the Soil, shall be
bound or liable, by virtue of such Apprenticeship, to
perform any Labour in the Service of his or her Employer
or Employers for more than Forty-five Hours in the whole
in any One Week.

Apprenticeship of the prædial Labourers not to continue beyond 1st August 1840;

VI. And be it further enacted, That no Person who by
virtue of this Act or of any such Act of Assembly, Ordinance, or Order in Council as aforesaid, shall become a
non-prædial apprenticed Labourer, shall continue in such
Apprenticeship beyond the First Day of *August* One
thousand eight hundred and thirty-eight.

of the non-prædial not beyond 1st August 1838.

VII. And be it further enacted, That if before any such
Apprenticeship shall have expired the Person or Persons
entitled for and during the Remainder of any such Term
to the Services of such apprenticed Labourer shall be

Before the Apprenticeship is expired, the Labourer may be discharged by his Employer.

desirous to discharge him or her from such Apprenticeship, it shall be lawful for such Person or Persons so to
do by any Deed or Instrument to be by him, her, or them
for that Purpose made and executed; which Deed or
Instrument shall be in such Form, and shall be executed
and recorded in such Manner and with such Solemnities,
as shall for that Purpose be prescribed under such
Authority, and in and by such Acts of Assembly, Ordi-
nances, or Orders in Council, as herein-after mentioned: *In case of Discharge of aged
or infirm La-
bourers, the
Employer to
be liable for
their Support.*
Provided nevertheless, that if any Person so discharged
from any such Apprenticeship by any such voluntary Act
as aforesaid shall at that Time be of the Age of Fifty Years
or upwards, or shall be then labouring under any such
Disease or mental or bodily Infirmity as may render him
or her incapable of earning his or her Subsistence, then and
in every such Case the Person or Persons so discharging
any such apprenticed Labourer as aforesaid shall continue
and be liable to provide for the Support and Maintenance
of such apprenticed Labourer during the remaining Term
of such original Apprenticeship, as fully as if such
apprenticed Labourer had not been discharged therefrom.

VIII. And be it further enacted, That it shall be lawful *Apprenticed
Labourer may
purchase his
Discharge
against the Will
of his Employ-
er, on an Ap-
praisement.*
for any such apprenticed Labourer to purchase his or her
Discharge from such Apprenticeship, even without the
Consent, or in opposition, if necessary, to the Will of the
Person or Persons entitled to his or her Services, upon
Payment to such Person or Persons of the appraised Value
of such Services; which Appraisement shall be effected,
and which Purchase Money shall be paid and applied, and
which Discharge shall be given and executed, in such
Manner and Form, and upon, under, and subject to such
Conditions, as shall be prescribed under such Authority,
and by such Acts of Assembly, Ordinances, or Orders in
Council, as are herein-after mentioned.

IX. And be it further enacted, That no apprenticed *Apprenticed
Labourers not
removable from
the Colony.*
Labourer shall be subject or liable to be removed from the
Colony to which he or she may belong; and that no
prædial apprenticed Labourer who may in Manner *Prædial apprenticed La-
bourers not re-
movable from
the Plantation
except by Con-
sent of Justices.*
aforesaid become attached to the Soil shall be subject or
liable to perform any Labour in the Service of his or her
Employer or Employers except upon or in or about the
Works and Business of the Plantations or Estates to which

such prædial apprenticed Labourer shall have been attached or on which he or she shall have been usually employed on or previously to the said First Day of *August* One thousand eight hundred and thirty-four: Provided nevertheless, that, with the Consent in Writing of any Two or more Justices of the Peace holding such Special Commission as herein-after mentioned, it shall be lawful for the Person or Persons entitled to the Services of any such attached prædial apprenticed Labourer or Labourers to transfer his or their Services to any other Estate or Plantation within the same Colony to such Person or Persons belonging; which written Consent shall in no Case be given, or be of any Validity, unless any such Justices of the Peace shall first have ascertained that such Transfer would not have the Effect of separating any such attached prædial apprenticed Labourer from his or her Wife or Husband, Parent or Child, or from any Person or Persons reputed to bear any such Relation to him or her, and that such Transfer would not probably be injurious to the Health or Welfare of such attached prædial apprenticed Labourer; and such written Consent to any such Removal shall be expressed in such Terms, and shall be in each Case given, attested, and recorded in such Manner, as shall for that Purpose be prescribed under such Authority, and by such Acts of Assembly, Ordinances, and Orders in Council, as herein-after mentioned.

Justices to ascertain that the Removal will not separate Members of Families.

X. And be it further enacted and declared, That the Right or Interest of any Employer or Employers to and in the Services of any such apprenticed Labourers as aforesaid shall pass and be transferable by Bargain and Sale, Contract, Deed, Conveyance, Will, or Descent, according to such Rules and in such Manner as shall for that Purpose be provided by any such Acts of Assembly, Ordinances, or Orders in Council as herein-after mentioned; provided that no such apprenticed Labourer shall, by virtue of any such Bargain and Sale, Contract, Deed, Conveyance, Will, or Descent, be subject or liable to be separated from his or her Wife or Husband, Parent or Child, or from any Person or Persons reputed to bear any such Relation to him or her.

Right to the Services to be transferable Property.

Labourer not to be separated from Wife, &c.

XI. And be it further enacted, That during the Continuance of any such Apprenticeship as aforesaid the

Employer to supply the Labourer with Food, &c.

Person or Persons for the Time being entitled to the Services of every such apprenticed Labourer shall be and is and are hereby required to supply him or her with such Food, Clothing, Lodging, Medicine, Medical Attendance, and such other Maintenance and Allowances as by any Law now in force in the Colony to which such apprenticed Labourer may belong an Owner is required to supply to and for any Slave being of the same Age and Sex as such apprenticed Labourer shall be; and in Cases in which the Food of any such prædial apprenticed Labourer shall be supplied, not by the Delivery to him or her of Provisions, but by the Cultivation by such prædial apprenticed Labourer of Ground set apart for the Growth of Provisions, the Person or Persons entitled to his or her Services shall and is or are hereby required to provide such prædial apprenticed Labourer with Ground adequate, both in Quantity and Quality, for his or her Support, and within a reasonable Distance of his or her usual Place of Abode, and to allow to such prædial apprenticed Labourer, from and out of the annual Time during which he or she may be required to labour, after the Rate of Forty five Hours *per* Week as aforesaid, in the Service of such his or her Employer or Employers, such a Portion of Time as shall be adequate for the proper Cultivation of such Ground, and for the raising and securing the Crops thereon grown; the actual Extent of which Ground, and the Distance thereof from the Place of Residence of the prædial apprenticed Labourer for whose Use it may be so allotted, and the Length of Time to be deducted for the Cultivation of the said Ground from the said annual Time, shall and may, in each of the Colonies aforesaid, be regulated under such Authorities, and by such Acts of Assembly, Ordinances, or Orders in Council as herein-after mentioned.

Where the prædial Labourer shall be maintained by the Cultivation of Provision Grounds, a proper Quantity of Ground with leisure Time to be set apart by the Employer.

How to be regulated.

XII. And be it further enacted, That, subject to the Obligations imposed by this Act, or to be imposed by any such Act of General Assembly, Ordinance, or Order in Council as herein-after mentioned, upon such apprenticed Labourers as aforesaid, all and every the Persons who on the said First Day of *August* One thousand eight hundred and thirty-four shall be holden in Slavery within any such *British* Colony as aforesaid shall upon and from and after

Subject to the Obligations imposed hereby, all Slaves in the British Colonies emancipated from the 1st August 1834.

the said First Day of *August* One thousand eight hundred and thirty-four become and be to all Intents and Purposes free and discharged of and from all Manner of Slavery, and shall be absolutely and for ever manumitted; and that the Children thereafter to be born to any such Persons, and the Offspring of such Children, shall in like Manner be free from their Birth; and that from and after the said First Day of *August* One thousand eight hundred and thirty-four Slavery shall be and is hereby utterly and for ever abolished and declared unlawful throughout the *British* Colonies, Plantations, and Possessions Abroad.

Children below the Age of Six on 1st August 1834, or born after that Time to any Female Apprentice, if destitute, may be bound out by any Special Magistrate as an Apprentice to the Person entitled to the Services of the Mother.

XIII. ' And whereas it may happen that Children who ' have not attained the Age of Six Years on the said First ' Day of *August* One thousand eight hundred and thirty- ' four, or that Children who after that Day may be born ' to any Female apprenticed Labourers, may not be ' properly supported by their Parents, and that no other ' Person may be disposed voluntarily to undertake the ' Support of such Children; and it is necessary that ' Provision should be made for the Maintenance of such ' Children in any such Contingency;' be it therefore enacted, That if any Child who on the said First Day of *August* One thousand eight hundred and thirty-four had not completed his or her Sixth Year, or if any Child to which any Female apprenticed Labourer may give birth on or after the said First Day of *August* One thousand eight hundred and thirty-four, shall be brought before any Justice of the Peace holding any such Special Commission as herein-after mentioned, and if it shall be made to appear to the Satisfaction of such Justice that any such Child is unprovided with an adequate Maintenance, and that such Child hath not completed his or her Age of Twelve Years, it shall be lawful for such Justice, and he is hereby required, on behalf of any such Child, to execute an Indenture of Apprenticeship, thereby binding such Child as an apprenticed Labourer to the Person or Persons entitled to the Services of the Mother of such Child, or who had been last entitled to the Services of such Mother; but in case it shall be made to appear to any such Justice that such Person or Persons aforesaid is or are unable or unfit to enter into such Indenture, and properly to perform the Conditions thereof, then it shall be lawful for such Justice and he is hereby required by such Indenture to bind any such Child to any other Person or Persons to be by him for that Purpose approved, and who may be willing and able properly to perform such Conditions; and it shall by every such Indenture of Apprenticeship be declared whether such Child shall thenceforward belong to the Class of attached prædial apprenticed Labourers, or to the Class of unattached prædial apprenticed Labourers, or to the Class of non-prædial apprenticed Labourers; and the Term of such Apprenticeship of any such Child shall by such Indenture be limited and made to continue in force until such Child shall have completed his or her Twenty-first Year, and no longer; and every Child so apprenticed as aforesaid by the Order of any such Justice of the Peace as aforesaid shall during his or her Apprenticeship be subject to all such and the same Rules and Regulations respecting the Work or Labour to be by them done or performed, and respecting the Food and other Supplies to be to him or her furnished, as any other such apprenticed Labourers as aforesaid: Provided always, that the said Indenture of Apprenticeship shall contain sufficient Words of Obligation upon the Employer to allow reasonable Time and Opportunity for the Education and Religious Instruction of such Child.

Indentures to continue in force until the Child has completed 21st Year.

XIV. And for ensuring the effectual Superintendence of the said apprenticed Labourers, and the Execution of this Act, be it enacted, That it shall and may be lawful for His Majesty to issue, or to authorize the Governor of any such Colony as aforesaid, in the Name and on the Behalf of His Majesty, to issue under the Public Seal of any such Colony, One or more Special Commission or Commissions to any One or more Person or Persons, constituting him or them a Justice or Justices of the Peace for the whole of any such Colony, or for any Parish, Precinct, Quarter, or other District within the same, for the special Purpose of giving effect to this present Act, and to any Laws which may, in manner herein-after mentioned, be made for giving more complete Effect to the same; and every Person to or in favour of whom any such Commission may be issued shall by force and virtue thereof, and without any other Qualification, be entitled and competent to act as a Justice of the Peace within the Limits prescribed by such

His Majesty, or any Governor by His Authority, may appoint Justices of the Peace by Special Commission to give effect to this Act.

Such Justices may also be included in the General Commission of the Peace.

his Commission for such special Purposes aforesaid, but for no other Purposes: Provided nevertheless, that nothing herein contained shall prevent or be construed to prevent any Person commissioned as a Justice of the Peace for such special Purpose as aforesaid from being included in the General Commission of the Peace for any such Colony, or for any Parish, Precinct, Quarter, or other District thereof, in case it shall seem fit to His Majesty, or to the Governor of any such Colony acting by His Majesty's Authority, to address both such Special Commission and such General Commission as aforesaid in any Case to the same Person or Persons.

His Majesty may grant Salaries to Special Justices.

XV. And be it further enacted, That His Majesty shall be and he is hereby authorized to grant to any Person or Persons, not exceeding One hundred in the whole, holding any such Special Commission or Commissions as aforesaid, and so from Time to Time as Vacancies may occur, Salaries at and after a Rate not exceeding in any Case the Sum of Three hundred Pounds Sterling *per Annum*, which Salary shall be payable so long only as any such Justice of the Peace shall retain any such Special Commission, and shall be actually resident in such Colony, and engaged in the Discharge of the Duties of such his Office; provided that no Person receiving or entitled to receive any Half Pay, Pension, or Allowance for or in respect of any past Services in His Majesty's Naval or Land Forces shall, by the Acceptance of any such Special Commission or Salary as aforesaid, forfeit or become incapable of receiving or lose his Right to receive such Half Pay, Pension, or Allowance, or any Part thereof, any Law, Statute, or Usage to the contrary in anywise notwithstanding: Provided also, that there be annually

Lists of such Persons to be laid before Parliament.

laid before both Houses of Parliament a List of the Names of all Persons to whom any such Salary shall be so granted, specifying the Date of every such Commission, and the Amount of the Salary assigned to every such Justice of the Peace.

Recital of various Regulations necessary for giving Effect to this Act.

XVI. ' And whereas it is necessary that various Rules ' and Regulations should be framed and established ' for ascertaining, with reference to each apprenticed ' Labourer within the said Colonies respectively, whether ' he or she belongs to the Class of attached prædial

' apprenticed Labourers, or to the Class of unattached
' apprenticed Labourers, or to the Class of non-prædial
' apprenticed Labourers, and for determining the Manner
' and Form in which and the Solemnities with which the
' voluntary Discharge of any apprenticed Labourer from
' such his or her Apprenticeship may be effected, and for
' prescribing the Form and Manner in which and the
' Solemnities with which the Purchase by any such
' apprenticed Labourer or his or her Discharge from such
' Apprenticeship without, or in opposition, if necessary,
' to, the Consent of the Person or Persons entitled to his or
' her Services, shall be effected, and how the necessary
' Appraisement of the future Value of such Services shall
' be made, and how and to whom the Amount of such
' Appraisement shall in each Case be paid and applied,
' and in what Manner and Form, and by whom the
' Discharge from any such Apprenticeship shall thereupon
' be given, executed, and recorded; and it is also necessary,
' for the Preservation of Peace throughout the said
' Colonies, that proper Regulations should be framed and
' established for the Maintenance of Order and good
' Discipline amongst the said apprenticed Labourers,
' and for ensuring the punctual Discharge of the Services
' due by them to their respective Employers, and for the
' Prevention and Punishment of Indolence, or the Neglect
' or improper Performance of Work by any such appren-
' ticed Labourer, and for enforcing the due Performance
' by any such apprenticed Labourer of any Contract into
' which he or she may voluntarily enter for any hired
' Service during the Time in which he or she may not be
' bound to labour for his or her Employer, and for the
' Prevention and Punishment of Insolence and Insubordi-
' nation on the Part of any such apprenticed Labourers
' towards their Employers, and for the Prevention or
' Punishment of Vagrancy or of any Conduct on the Part
' of any such apprenticed Labourers injuring or tending to
' the Injury of the Property of any such Employer, and
' for the Suppression and Punishment of any Riot or
' combined Resistance of the Laws on the Part of any such
' apprenticed Labourers, and for preventing the Escape
' of any such apprenticed Labourers, during their Term
' of Apprenticeship, from the Colonies to which they may

' respectively belong: And whereas it will also be necessary
' for the Protection of such apprenticed Labourers as
' aforesaid that various Regulations should be framed and
' established in the said respective Colonies for securing
' Punctuality and Method in the Supply to them of such
' Food, Clothing, Lodging, Medicines, Medical Atten-
' dance, and such other Maintenance and Allowances as
' they are herein-before declared entitled to receive, and
' for regulating the Amount and Quality of all such Articles
' in Cases where the Laws at present existing in any such
' Colony may not in the Case of Slaves have made any
' Regulation or any adequate Regulation for that Purpose;
' and it is also necessary that proper Rules should be
' established for the Prevention and Punishment of any
' Frauds which might be practised, or of any Omissions or
' Neglects which might occur, respecting the Quantity
' or the Quality of the Supplies so to be furnished, or
' respecting the Periods for the Delivery of the same:
' And whereas it is necessary, in those Cases in which the
' Food of any such prædial apprenticed Labourers as
' aforesaid may either wholly or in part be raised by
' themselves by the Cultivation of Ground to be set apart
' and allotted for that Purpose, that proper Regulations
' should be made and established as to the Extent of such
' Grounds, and as to the Distance at which such Grounds
' may be so allotted from the ordinary Place of Abode of
' such prædial apprenticed Labourers, and respecting the
' Deductions to be made from the Cultivation of such
' Grounds from the annual Time during which such
' prædial apprenticed Labourers are herein-before declared
' liable to labour: And whereas it may also be necessary,
' by such Regulations as aforesaid, to secure to the said
' prædial apprenticed Labourers the Enjoyment for their
' own Benefit of that Portion of their Time during which
' they are not hereby required to labour in the Service of
' their respective Employers, and for securing Exactness
' in the Computation of the Time during which such
' prædial apprenticed Labourers are hereby required to
' labour in the Service of such their respective Employers;
' and it is also necessary that Provision should be made for
' preventing the Imposition of Task-work on any such
' apprenticed Labourer without his or her free Consent to

' undertake the same; but it may be necessary by such
' Regulations in certain Cases to require and provide for
' the Acquiescence of the Minority of the prædial
' apprenticed Labourers attached to any Plantation or
' Estate in the Distribution and Apportionment amongst
' the whole Body of such Labourers of any Task-work
' which the Majority of such Body shall be willing and
' desirous collectively to undertake, and it is also necessary
' that Regulations should be made respecting any voluntary
' Contracts into which any apprenticed Labourers may
' enter with their respective Employers or with any other
' Person for hired Service for any future Period, and for
' limiting the greatest Period of Time to which such volun-
' tary Contract may extend, and for enforcing the punctual
' and effectual Performance of such voluntary Contracts
' on the Part both of such apprenticed Labourers and of
' the Person or Persons engaging for their Employment
' and Hire; and it is also necessary that Regulations should
' be made for the Prevention or Punishment of any Cruelty,
' Injustice, or other Wrong or Injury which may be done
' to or inflicted upon any such apprenticed Labourers by
' the Persons entitled to their Services; and it is also
' necessary that proper Regulations should be made
' respecting the Manner and Form in which such Inden-
' tures of Apprenticeship as aforesaid shall be made on
' behalf of such Children as aforesaid, and respecting the
' registering and Preservation of all such Indentures: And
' whereas it is also necessary that Provision should be
' made for ensuring Promptitude and Dispatch, and for
' preventing all unnecessary Expence, in the Discharge
' by the Justices of the Peace holding such Special Com-
' missions as aforesaid of the Jurisdiction and Authorities
' thereby committed to them, and for enabling such
' Justices to decide in a summary Way such Questions
' as may be brought before them in that Capacity, and for
' the Division of the said respective Colonies into Districts
' for the Purposes of such Jurisdiction, and for the frequent
' and punctual Visitation by such Justices of the Peace
' of the apprenticed Labourers within such their respective
' Districts; and it is also necessary that Regulations should
' be made for indemnifying and protecting such Justices
' of the Peace in the upright Execution and Discharge of

' their Duties: And whereas such Regulations as aforesaid
' could not without great Inconvenience be made except
' by the respective Governors, Councils, and Assemblies,
' or other local Legislatures of the said respective Colonies,

This Act not to prevent the Enactment by His Majesty in Council, of the Laws necessary for establishing such Regulations.

' or by His Majesty, with the Advice of His Privy Council,
' in reference to those Colonies to which the Legislative
' Authority of His Majesty in Council extends:' Be it
therefore enacted and declared, That nothing in this Act
contained extends or shall be construed to extend to
prevent the Enactment by the respective Governors,
Councils, and Assemblies, or by such other local Legislatures as aforesaid, or by His Majesty, with the Advice of
His Privy Council, of any such Acts of General Assembly,
or Ordinances, or Orders in Council as may be requisite
for making and establishing such several Rules and
Regulations as aforesaid, or any of them, or for carrying
the same or any of them into full and complete Effect:

Provisions re-
pugnant to this
Act contained
in any such
Colonial Law
void.

Provided nevertheless, that it shall not be lawful for any
such Governor, Council, and Assembly, or for any such
local Legislature, or for His Majesty in Council, by any
such Acts of Assembly, Ordinances, or Orders in Council
as aforesaid, to make or establish any Enactment, Regulation, Provision, Rule, or Order which shall be in anywise
repugnant or contradictory to this present Act or any Part
thereof, but that every such Enactment, Regulation,
Provision, Rule, or Order shall be and is hereby declared
to be absolutely null and void and of no effect.

Such Colonial
Acts may not
authorize the
whipping or
other Punish-
ment of the
Labourer by
the Employer's
Authority.

XVII. Provided also, and be it further enacted, That
it shall not be lawful for any such Governor, Council, and
Assembly, or other Colonial Legislature, or for His
Majesty in Council, by any such Act, Ordinance, or
Order in Council, to authorize any Person or Persons
entitled to the Services of any such apprenticed Labourer,
or any other Person or Persons other than such Justices of
the Peace holding such Special Commissions as aforesaid,
to punish any such apprenticed Labourer for any Offence
by him or her committed or alleged to have been committed
by the whipping, beating, or Imprisonment of his or her
Person, or by any other personal or other Correction or
Punishment whatsoever, or by any Addition to the Hours
of Labour herein-before limited; nor to authorize any
Court, Judge, or Justice of the Peace to punish any such

apprenticed Labourer, being a Female, for any Offence by her committed, by whipping or beating her Person; and that every Enactment, Regulation, Provision, Rule, or Order for any such Purpose in any such Act, Ordinance, or Order in Council contained shall be and is hereby declared to be absolutely null and void and of no effect: Provided always, that nothing in this Act contained doth or shall extend to exempt any apprenticed Labourer in any of the said Colonies from the Operation of any Law or Police Regulation which is or shall be in force therein for the Prevention or Punishment of any Offence, such Law or Police Regulation being in force against and applicable to all other Persons of free Condition.

XVIII. Provided also, and be it further enacted, That it shall not be lawful for any such Governor, Council, and Assembly, or for any such local Legislature, or for His Majesty in Council, by any such Acts of General Assembly, Ordinances, or Orders in Council as aforesaid, to authorize any Magistrate or Justice of the Peace, other than and except the Justices of the Peace holding such Special Commissions as aforesaid, to take cognizance of any Offence committed or alleged to have been committed by any such apprenticed Labourer, or by his or her Employer, in such their Relation to each other, or of the Breach, Violation, or Neglect of any of the Obligations owed by them to each other, or of any Question, Matter, or Thing incident to or arising out of the Relations subsisting between such apprenticed Labourers and the Persons respectively entitled to their Services; and every Enactment, Regulation, Provision, Rule, or Order in any such Acts, Ordinances, and Orders in Council to the contrary contained shall be and is hereby declared to be null and void and of no effect. . . .

Colonial Acts or Orders in Council not to authorize any Justices, except those having Special Commissions, to act in execution thereof.

XXIV. And whereas, towards compensating the persons at present entitled to the services if the slaves to be manumitted and set free by virtue of this Act for the loss of such Services, His Majesty's most dutiful and loyal subjects the Commons of Great Britain and Ireland in Parliament assembled have resolved to give and grant to His Majesty the Sum of Twenty Millions Pounds Sterling; be it enacted, That the Lords Commissioners of His Majesty's Treasury of the United Kingdom of Great

Britain and Ireland may raise such Sum or Sums of Money as shall be required from Time to Time under the Provisions of this Act, and may grant as the Consideration for such Sum or Sums of Money Redeemable Perpetual Annuities or Annuities for Terms of Years (which said Annuities respectively shall be transferable and payable at the Bank of *England*), upon such Terms and Conditions and under such Regulations as to the Time or Times of paying the said Sums of Money agreed to be raised as may be determined upon by the said Commissioners of the Treasury, not exceeding in the whole the Sum of Twenty Millions Pounds Sterling: Provided nevertheless, that the Rate of Interest at which the said Sums of Money shall be from Time to Time raised shall be regulated and governed by the Price of the respective Redeemable Perpetual Annuities or Annuities for Terms of Years on the Day preceding (or on the nearest preceding Day if it shall so happen that there shall be no Price of such said Annuities respectively on the Day immediately preceding) the Day of giving Notice for raising, such Sum or Sums of Money, and that the Rate of Interest to be allowed to the Contributors for such Sum or Sums of Money shall in no Case exceed Five Shillings *per Centum per Annum* above the current Rate of Interest produced by the Market Price of any such Redeemable Perpetual Annuities or Annuities for Terms of Years existing at the Time, and in which such Contracts shall be made. . . .

LV. And be it further enacted, That any Person having or Claiming to have had any Right, Title, or Interest in or to, or any Mortgage, Judgment, Charge, Incumbrance, or other Lien upon, any Slave or Slaves so to be manumitted as aforesaid, at the Time of such their Manumission, shall and may prefer such Claims before the said Commissioners; and for ensuring Method, Regularity, and Dispatch in the Mode of preferring and of proceeding upon such Claims, the said Commissioners shall and are hereby authorized by general Rules, to be framed and published, confirmed, allowed, and inrolled as aforesaid, to prescribe the Form and Manner of Proceeding to be observed by any Claimant or Claimants preferring any such Claims, and to authorize the Assistant Commissioners so to be appointed in the said several Colonies to receive

Persons interested in any Slaves manumitted by this Act may prefer Claims before the Commissioners, who are to make Rules for the Conduct of all Proceedings under the Commission.

and report upon the same or any of them in such Manner and Form and under such Regulations as to the Commissioners so to be appointed by His Majesty as aforesaid shall seem meet, and to prescribe the Manner, the Time or Times, the Place or Places, and the Form or Forms in which Notices of such Claims shall be published for general Information, or especially communicated to or served upon any Person or Persons interested therein or affected thereby, and to prescribe the Form and Manner of Proceeding to be observed upon the Prosecution of such Claims, or in making any Opposition to the same, and to make all such Regulations as to them may seem best adapted for promoting Method, Economy, and Dispatch in the Investigation of such Claims, and respecting the Evidence to be taken and admitted for or against the same, and respecting the Manner and Form of adjudicating thereupon, and otherwise how ever respecting the Method, Form, and Manner of Proceeding to be observed either by them the said Assistant Commissioners, or by the Parties to any Proceedings before them, their Agents or Witnesses, and which Rules shall from Time to Time be liable to be amended, altered, varied, or renewed as Occasion may require, in such Manner as is herein-before directed. . . .

LXIV. And be it further enacted, That nothing in this Act contained doth or shall extend to any of the Territories in the Possession of the *East India* Company, or to the Island of *Ceylon*, or to the Island of *Saint Helena*. *Act not to extend to East Indies, &c.*

LXV. And be it further enacted that in the Colonies of the Cape of Good Hope and Mauritius, the several parts of this Act shall take effect and come into operation, or shall cease to operate and to be in force, as the case may be, at periods more remote than the respective periods herein before such Purposes limited by the following intervals of time, *videlicit* by four calendar months in the Colony of the Cape of Good Hope, and six calendar months in the Colony of Mauritius.

LXVI. And be it further enacted and declared that within the meaning and for the purpose of this Act all islands and Territories dependent upon any of the Colonies aforesaid and constituting Parts of the same Colonial Government, shall respectively be taken to be parts of such respective Colonies.

11. FROM a Letter of Thomas Clarkson to William Smith, 1 September 1833 (William Smith Papers, Perkins Library, Duke University)*

... And now we have both of us lived to see those two great days for our country, and for humanity, the abolition of the slave trade, and of W. Indian or rather colonial slavery. Having seen this we may depart in peace; for we may leave the world with an assurance, that slavery has now received what will be its death blow in every part of the world. This is what I never thought either of us would have lived to see, nor thought we would have had this superlative, this overwhelming pleasure, had it not been for the administration of Lord Grey. The more I think of what has been done, the more I am astonished, and at the same time grateful. The twenty millions will have been well laid out, if it will secure the cordial cooperation of the planters in the great work. It is not to be thought of for a moment, if we consider the evils, both physical and moral, from which both slaves and the masters have been delivered, and to what extent. I wish the apprenticeship had been two years shorter. But we cannot always have what we wish. The subject was one of extraordinary difficulty, opposite and conflicting interests were to be reconciled, dangers of the first magnitude were to be apprehended and yet guarded against. I am truly thankful that the thing has been so well got over. But to return. We may both of us, as I said before, depart in peace; for our eyes have seen a great salvation, and we have had a hand in it too. But alas, how few are now alive of those who begun the work! of the old committee only Richard Phillips and myself now remain; of the original parliamentary labourers (Wilberforce being dead) you only are left. I have just had read to me a very pretty, and sensible letter of yours dated June 1, 1787, to our committee on the subject of its institution; and now for another subject.

The two committees must close their accounts, get their debts paid, and *be disbanded*—and another, on a frugal *and less expensive office* and a less number of servants be *instituted*, on the plan of the African Institution, which followed the abolition of the slave trade, to keep a

---

* Quoted by permission.

watch over the execution of the last bill, by establishing correspondents in the W. Indies, taking in W. I. Gazettes, thus learning all that passes there, and acting accordingly. It would be the office of this Institution to wait upon government, with information, and give also information to the people of England, of what happens in the Colonies, favourable or adverse. But then this committee ought to be a very prudent, and discreet committee; among those, who ought not to be in it, are the two (whoever they may be) who posted Buxton. Such men ought not to belong to any committee entrusted with a great cause, where prudence ought to be a virtue.

I have just room to send my kind regards to Mrs Smith.

Yours affectionately
Thomas Clarkson

INDEX

African 19, 25, 26, 27, 28, 29, 39, 94, 104, 110
African Institution 29, 174
Agency Committee 37, 49, 50, 51, 54, 60, 74, 83, 91, 126
Althorp, Lord 52, 56, 57, 58, 61, 64
Anglican Church 19, 72, 80, 81, 86, 87
Anglicans 17, 18, 82, 93, 95, 96
Anti-Slavery Movement 9, 15, 16, 20, 22, 27, 29, 36, 42–3, 46, 51, 54, 60, 65, 69; — and Dissenters 17–19, 24, 82–5, 88, 93, 96; — London Committee 32, 50, 54, 72; — Mass Demonstrations 61, 75, 90; — and Women 88–92; — Leadership 32, 36, 49, 50, 81, 94
Anti-Slavery Reporter 33, 90–1, 129
Apprenticeship 63, 65, 66, 67, 68, 70, 71(n), 73, 74, 75, 76, 83, 84, 159, 160–3, 165, 167, 171

Baldwin, George 127
Baptists 17, 24, 26, 43, 50, 53, 80, 81, 84
Barbados 29, 41, 76, 77
Barrett, Richard 64(n), 87(n)
Bathurst, Earl 32, 124
Benezet, Anthony 24, 27, 28, 29
Berkshire 56, 57, 84
Bible 17, 21, 44, 45
Birmingham 53, 68, 69, 74, 84, 92
Blackstone, William 26
Booth, Abraham 24, 25
Borthwick, Peter 133, 134, 135, 136, 137
British Empire 9, 17, 19, 29, 76, 92, 95, 97, 151
British and Foreign Anti-Slavery Society (BFASS) 93, 94, 95
British North America 73(n)
British Society 15, 16, 21, 65, 77
Brougham, Lord (Henry) 10, 34, 75, 94
Buckingham 55, 56, 57, 62(n), 69
Buxton, Sir Thomas Fowell 10, 19, 30, 31, 51, 52, 55, 57, 58, 59, 60, 65, 66, 67, 69, 70, 71, 72(n), 74, 83, 84, 95, 96

Canterbury, Archbishop of 51(n)
Cape of Good Hope 73(n), 74, 173
Central Emancipation Committee 74, 75, 76
Ceylon 72(n), 173
Chandos, Marquis of 84
Chartered Colonies 113, 114, 115
Christian 15, 17, 19, 35, 42, 79, 80, 85, 92, 96
Clapham Sect 17
Clarkson, Thomas 9, 10, 25, 27, 40, 71(n), 73, 74(n), 127, 174, 175
Colonies 17, 23, 31, 32, 33, 34, 41, 53, 74
Colonial Legislatures 31
Cobbett, William 61(n), 64
Compensation 61, 63, 64, 65, 69, 70, 71(n), 88, 118, 172–3
Canning, George 31, 34, 149, 151
Cropper, James 50, 70
Crown Colonies 76, 113, 114, 115

Davis, David Brion 16, 22(n)
Dewdney, Rev. E. 127
Dickson, William 29
Dissenters 17, 18, 19, 24, 30, 42, 43, 50, 54, 55, 56, 71, 81, 82, 83, 84, 85, 88, 92, 93, 96, 131; — Committee of Deputies 85, 86
Dublin 67(n), 94

East Indian Charter Bill (1833) 72
East Indian Slavery, see Slavery
Edinburgh 92, 94
Eighteenth century 15, 17, 25, 27
Ellenborough, Lord 87
Emancipation 9, 18, 19, 26, 29, 30, 33, 35, 37, 39, 50, 56, 58, 59, 62, 66, 67, 71–3, 85, 86(n), 138, 145, 153; — Gradual 30–3; — Immediate 30, 32, 36, 56, 61, 65, 66, 128; — Government proposals 63–6; — Act of 1833 67, 76, 87, 96, 97, 158–73; — Universal 74, 94–5
Evangelical 40, 43, 46, 74, 82, 92–3, 96; — Revival 17–18, 23, 79, 80

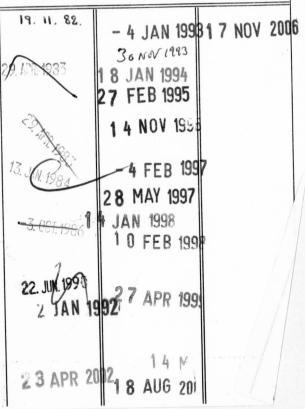